Recom

WAYSIDE INNS
OF BRITAIN
1991

Recommended
WAYSIDE INNS
OF BRITAIN
1991

A Selection of Hostelries of Character
for Food and Drink and in many cases,
Accommodation

Editorial Consultant
PETER STANLEY WILLIAMS

FHG PUBLICATIONS

Other FHG Publications 1991

Recommended Country Hotels of Britain
Recommended Wayside Inns of Britain
Recommended Short Break Holidays in Britain
Pets Welcome!
Bed and Breakfast in Britain
The Golf Guide: Where to Play/Where to Stay

1991 Edition
ISBN 1 85055 130 8
© FHG Publications Ltd.
No part of this publication may be reproduced by any means or
transmitted without the permission of the Publishers.

Cartography by GEO projects (U.K.) Ltd., Henley-on-Thames
Maps are based on Ordnance Survey maps with the permission of
the Controller of Her Majesty's Stationery Office. Crown copyright reserved.

Typeset by R D Composition Ltd., Glasgow.
Printed and bound in Great Britain by Richard Clays, Bungay, Suffolk.

Distribution. **Book Trade:** Moorland Publishing, Moor Farm Road, Ashbourne, Derbyshire DE6 1HD (Tel: 0335
44486. Fax: 0335 46397). **News Trade:** UMD, 1 Benwell Road, Holloway, London N7 7AX (Tel: 071-700 4600.
Fax: 071-607 3352).

Published by FHG Publications Ltd.
Abbey Mill Business Centre, Seedhill, Paisley PA1 1JN (041-887 0428).
A member of the U.N. Group.

Cover design: Edward Carden (Glasgow)
Cover picture: Red Lion Inn, New Forest (Vic Guy)

———————

US ISBN 1-55650-288-5
Distributed in the United States by
Hunter Publishing Inc., 300 Raritan Center Parkway, CN94,
Edison, N.J., 08818, USA

CONTENTS

Wayside Inns

ENGLAND

LOCATION OF INNS

(Alphabetical list of Towns/Villages)

Abbotsbury, DORSET 53
Acaster Malbis, NORTH YORKS 124
Aldham, ESSEX 58
Alfriston, E SUSSEX 109
Almondsbury, AVON 12
Appleby-in-Westmorland, CUMBRIA 28
Arundel, W SUSSEX 111
Askham, CUMBRIA 28
Askrigg, NORTH YORKS 123
Aston Crews, HEREFORD 71
Aust, AVON 11
Axmouth, DEVON 41
Bainbridge, NORTH YORKS 124
Bamford, DERBY 37
Barbon, LANCS 77
Barngates, CUMBRIA 29
Barnsley, GLOUCS 60
Beaconsfield, BUCKS 15
Beauworth, HANTS 66
Beer, DEVON 41
Belford, N'UMBERLAND 86
Bewdley, WORCS 121
Birdlip, GLOUCS 60
Bishop Wilton, HUMBERSIDE 73
Blandford, DORSET 54
Bledington, OXON 89
Blockley, GLOUCS 61
Bodinnick-by-Fowey, CORNWALL 23
Bollington, CHES 20
Boston Spa, WEST YORKS 132
Boston, LINCS 79
Bourton, DORSET 54
Bourton-on-the-Water, GLOUCS 61
Bowland Bridge, CUMBRIA 30
Braithwaite, CUMBRIA 30
Brampton, CUMBRIA 31
Bredwardine, HEREFORD 71
Brierley Hill, W MIDLANDS 115
Buckden, CAMBS 18
Buckden, NORTH YORKS 125
Buckfastleigh, DEVON 42

Burford, OXON 89
Burnham Market, NORFOLK 81
Burnham-on-Crouch, ESSEX 58
Burrow-with-Burrow, CUMBRIA 32
Cannington, SOMERSET 96
Canterbury, KENT 75
Cardington, SHROPSHIRE 94
Castle Cary, SOMERSET 97
Castleton, DERBY 38
Chale, I.O.WIGHT 74
Charlbury, OXON 90
Cheriton Bishop, DEVON 42
Chiddingfold, SURREY 106
Chideock, DORSET 54
Chipperfield, HERTS 73
Chislehampton, OXON 90
Chudleigh Knighton, DEVON 42
Clapham, NORTH YORKS 125
Clare, SUFFOLK 102
Clayton, W SUSSEX 111
Clovelly, DEVON 43
Coleford, DEVON 43
Colesbourne, GLOUCS 61
Coniston, CUMBRIA 31
Constantine, CORNWALL 23
Countisbury DEVON 43
Cracoe, NORTH YORKS 125
Cray, NORTH YORKS 126
Crewkerne, SOMERSET 97
Dallington, E SUSSEX 110
Dalwood, DEVON 44
Damerham, HANTS 66
Dartington, DEVON 44
Dartmouth, DEVON 45
Dereham, NORFOLK 81
Devizes, WILTS 116
Doddiscombsleigh, DEVON 46
Dunstan, N'UMBERLAND 87
East Ilsley, BERKS 14
Eastling, KENT 76
Edale, SOUTH YORKS 131

Egton Bridge, NORTH YORKS 126
Elslack, NORTH YORKS 127
Elstead, SURREY 106
Elsted, W SUSSEX 112
Elterwater, CUMBRIA 32
Eltisley, CAMBS 19
Emery Down, HANTS 67
Ettington, WARWICKS 114
Ewen, GLOUCS 62
Exford, SOMERSET 98
Fladbury, WORCS 122
Fonthill Gifford, WILTS 117
Ford, WILTS 117
Fownhope, HEREFORD 71
Framlingham, SUFFOLK 103
Freeland, OXON 90
Froggatt Edge, DERBY 38
Georgeham, DEVON 47
Godalming, SURREY 107
Great Barrington, GLOUCS 62
Great Brickhill, BUCKS 16
Great Ryburgh, NORFOLK 83
Great Wishford, WILTS 118
Hadley Heath, WORCS 122
Halford, WARWICKS 115
Hanley Castle, WORCS 122
Hascombe, SURREY 108
Hatherleigh, DEVON 47
Hawkshead, CUMBRIA 33
Hexworthy, DEVON 47
Higher Burwardsley, CHESHIRE 21
Holbeach, LINCS 79
Holmrook, CUMBRIA 33
Holywell, CAMBS 19
Hopton Wafers, SHROPSHIRE 95
Horam, E SUSSEX 110
Horns Cross, DEVON 48
Hough-on-the-Hill, LINCS 79
Huby, NORTH YORKS 128
Hurtmore, SURREY 108
Kilburn, NORTH YORKS 128
Kilmington, WILTS 118
King's Nympton, DEVON 48
Kings Worthy, HANTS 67
Kingsbridge, DEVON 49
Kingsteignton, DEVON 49
Kinver, W MIDLANDS 116
Kirkwhelpington, N'UMBERLAND 87
Lanreath, CORNWALL 24
Lavenham, SUFFOLK 103

Leadenham, LINCS 80
Leafield, OXON 90
Ledbury, HEREFORD 71
Leek, STAFFS 101
Leverington, CAMBS 20
Lewdown, DEVON 49
Linwood, HANTS 67
London 80
Long Melford, SUFFOLK 103
Longframlington, N'UMBERLAND 87
Lostwithiel, CORNWALL 24
Loweswater, CUMBRIA 34
Ludlow, SHROPSHIRE 95
Lyddington, LANCS 78
Lynmouth, DEVON 50
Lynton, DEVON 50
Maidenhead, BERKS 15
Matlock, DERBY 39
Mayfield, E SUSSEX 110
Menheniot, CORNWALL 24
Middleton in Teesdale,
  CO. DURHAM 56
Minster Lovell, OXON 91
Monkton Combe, AVON 12
Much Wenlock, SHROPSHIRE 96
Mungrisdale, CUMBRIA 34
Neatishead, NORFOLK 82
Nettleton, WILTS 119
North Gorley, HANTS 68
North Nibley, GLOUCS 63
Nunney, SOMERSET 98
Nuthurst, W SUSSEX 112
Odiham, HANTS 68
Onneley, STAFFS 102
Orford, SUFFOLK 104
Over Haddon, DERBY 39
Owlsebury, HANTS 68
Pagham, W SUSSEX 112
Parracombe, DEVON 51
Pelynt, CORNWALL 25
Penrith, CUMBRIA 35
Pickering, NORTH YORKS 129
Piercebridge, NORTH YORKS 129
Pillaton, CORNWALL 25
Powerstock, DORSET 55
Ravendale, CUMBRIA 35
Reedham, NORFOLK 83
Ripon, NORTH YORKS 129
Rowsley, DERBY 39
Running Waters, CO. DURHAM 57

Salisbury, WILTS 119
Sandbach, CHESHIRE 21
Saunderton, BUCKS 16
Scarborough, NORTH YORKS 130
Scole, NORFOLK 84
Seahouses, N'UMBERLAND 88
Sedgefield, CO. DURHAM 57
Shenington, OXON 91
Shipton-under-Wychwood, OXON 92
Skirmett, OXON 91
Slaidburn, LANCS 78
Southwold, SUFFOLK 105
St Agnes, CORNWALL 26
St Briavels, GLOUCS 63
St Ewe, CORNWALL 26
St Mary Bourne, HANTS 70
St Teath, CORNWALL 27
Stanbury, WEST YORKS 132
Steyning, W SUSSEX 113
Stockbridge, HANTS 69
Stow Bardolph, NORFOLK 83
Stow-on-the-Wold, GLOUCS 64
Stratfield Turgis, HANTS 70
Stretton, LANCS 78
Sulgrave, NORTHANTS 86
Sulgrave, OXON 93
Sutton Staithe, NORFOLK 85
Sutton, CHESHIRE 22
Swinscoe, DERBY 40
Symonds Yat West, HEREFORD 72
Talkin, CUMBRIA 35
Tarrant Monkton, DORSET 55
Thame, OXON 93
Thornham Magna, SUFFOLK 105
Thornham, NORFOLK 85
Thornton Watlass, NORTH YORKS 130
Tideswell, DERBY 40
Tivetshall St Mary, NORFOLK 85
Tormarton, AVON 13
Torquay, DEVON 52
Torver, CUMBRIA 36
Totnes, DEVON 52
Trebarwith, CORNWALL 27
Twyford, BERKS 14
Ugborough, DEVON 53
Upper Oddington, GLOUCS 65
Upton-upon-Severn, WORCS 123
Walbottle, TYNE & WEAR 113
Wall, N'UMBERLAND 88
Wark-on-Tyne, N'UMBERLAND 88

Warminster, WILTS 120
Warren Street, KENT 76
Warwick-on-Eden, CUMBRIA 36
Wasdale Head, CUMBRIA 36
Watchet, SOMERSET 99
Wells-next-the-Sea, NORFOLK 86
Wendover, BUCKS 16
West Witton, NORTH YORKS 131
Willingham, CAMBS 20
Williton, SOMERSET 100
Winton, CUMBRIA 36
Withypool, SOMERSET 100
Wooburn Common, BUCKS 17
Wootton Rivers, WILTS 121
Wotton-under-Edge, GLOUCS 65
Wrotham, KENT 77

WALES

Beaumaris, GWYNEDD 137
Builth Wells, POWYS 139
Capel Garmon, GWYNEDD 138
Llanarmon, CLWYD 134
Llanarthney, DYFED 135
Llanbedr-Y-Cennin, GWYNEDD 138
Llanefydd, CLWYD 133
Llansilin, CLWYD 133
Nevern, DYFED 136
Nolton Haven, DYFED 136
Presteigne, POWYS 140
Rhandirmwyn, DYFED 137
Trefor, GWYNEDD 139
Tretower, POWYS 140

SCOTLAND

Achnasheen, ROSS-SHIRE 154
Auchtermuchty, FIFE 145
Bothwell, LANARK 151
Bridge of Cally, PERTH 153
Cairndow, ARGYLL 141
Chirnside, BERWICK 143
Dundonnell, ROSS-SHIRE 155
Easdale, ARGYLL 142
Fortrose, ROSS-SHIRE 155
Freuchie, FIFE 146
Gairloch, ROSS-SHIRE 155

Recommended WAYSIDE INNS OF BRITAIN 1991

THE WARMEST WELCOME

Whoe'er has travell'd life's dull round
Where'er his stages may have been,
May sigh to think he still has found
The warmest welcome at an inn

William Shenstone, 1714-1763

There is nothing like the British inn elsewhere in the world: it expresses the very character of the people. Those, particularly of the wayside or rural variety, are very much a way of life, so firmly embedded and interwoven into the landscape as to be a feature of the surrounding countryside. Apart from being centres of pride and affection for the local community, they are focal points of abounding interest for the tourist of today who will, invariably, be rewarded by a cheerful atmosphere, convivial company and good refreshment. I say 'invariably' because, even with sophisticated improvements in standards of comfort, catering and accommodation and the re-emergence of real ale, the eager seeker still needs advice. "Word-of-mouth" recommendation is usually a sound recipe for satisfaction but is often very local in reference and limited in scope.

Recommended WAYSIDE INNS OF BRITAIN is a "word of pen" collection of recommendations to hostelries of character all over Britain which the publishers and myself are confident meet the prerequisites of a visit to remember. Most of the inns featured in this hedonists' essential work of reference are situated in pleasant, occasionally idyllic, surroundings. Some are large, some small and homely; many are of great historic and architectural interest; some cater for overnight guests, some do not – there is a wide choice.

One thing they all have in common, however, is the ability to please, sustain and satisfy in the way traditional to the British inn over the centuries. Although the publishers cannot accept responsibility for any errors or omissions from the following descriptions, they are published in good faith in the belief that the experiences gained will be supremely enjoyable.

It is not necessary to travel far in search of the "warmest welcome" but wherever fancy may fly, I wish our readers "good cheer" in the hope that this book will fulfil its purpose.

Peter Stanley Williams
Editorial Consultant

Avon

BOAR'S HEAD,
Aust, Near Bristol,
Avon BS12 3AX

Tel: 045-45 2278

No accommodation; Dinners (Thursday, Friday, Saturday) and snacks; Car park (25);
Bristol 13 miles, Thornbury 4.

For rewarding relaxation, momentary or extended, leave the nearby M4 (Junction 21), ignoring the Severn Bridge, and turn down to the generally disregarded village of Aust and this charming 17th century inn with its big open fireplace and stone walls. A stone heart it certainly does not have as we soon found out. We were confronted by a smiling welcome and an appetising selection of home-made dishes with the option of choosing from a vast buffet menu (Monday-Friday). The meal, drinks and service were excellent and the children had a wonderful time in the garden with its rabbits, guinea pigs, climbing frame and swing. We found it hard to leave.

NOTE

All the information in this book is given in good faith in the belief that it is correct. However, the publishers cannot guarantee the facts given in these pages, neither are they responsible for changes in policy, ownership or terms that may take place after the date of going to press. Readers should always satisfy themselves that the facilities they require are available and that the terms, if quoted, still apply.

BOWL INN AND RESTAURANT,
16 Church Road, Lower Almondsbury,
Bristol, Avon BS12 4DT

Tel: 0454 612757/613717

Accommodation (2 bedrooms, both with private bathroom); Historic interest; Luncheons, dinners (not Sundays) and snacks; Car park; Bristol 7 miles.

One has a certain sympathy with the ghost of the Gray Lady which is said to haunt this hostelry — for anyone would be reluctant to leave the whitewashed Bowl Inn which overlooks the Severn Estuary from its quiet corner of the Vale. Bar food here includes homemade soup and sandwiches, fresh or toasted, together with a wide range of other snacks and meals, such as chilli, lamb stew, lasagne and tastily filled pies, and more formal cuisine is available in the restaurant which boasts an extensive à la carte menu. Overnight accommodation is tucked away in "The Cottage", just down the road. *Les Routiers.*

THE WHEELWRIGHTS ARMS,
Monkton Combe, Near Bath,
Avon BA2 7HD

4 Tel: 0225-72 2287

Accommodation (8 bedrooms, all with private shower); Free house; Historic interest; Luncheons, grills and snacks; Car park (20); Bath 3 miles.

With excellent accommodation housed in the converted barn and stables, this is a lovely base from which to visit the numerous houses, gardens and places of interest which lie within a few miles, including of course the city of Bath itself. The hostelry stands in the peace and quiet of the lovely Midford valley. A large selection of home cooked food is served, with the addition of a grill menu in the evening. In addition there is a choice of four real ales. The bedrooms (mostly beamed) are equipped with shower, toilet, washbasin, colour television, central heating, tea and coffee making facilities, direct-dial telephones and hairdryers. Terms are very reasonable. The inn is also a lovely base for walking, fishing, riding or just relaxing. In the summer guests are free to use the pleasant garden and patio, and in winter cosy log fires warm the bar.

COMPASS INN,
Tormarton, Near Badminton,
Avon GL9 1JB

Tel: 045-421 242

Fax: 045-421 741

Accommodation (32 bedrooms, all with private bathroom); Free house; Dinners and snacks; Car park (100); Chipping Sodbury 3 miles.

A traditional establishment in which modern comforts and amenities have been unobtrusively incorporated, the Compass stands in its own six acres of ground, well situated for visiting the Cotswolds, Bath and Bristol as well as being easily accessible from the M4 and 5. Thirty-two bedrooms serve overnight guests, all having pleasing decor and furnishings and their own private bath or shower, in addition to colour television, direct-dial telephone and facilities for making tea and coffee. Several cosy beamed bars offer a choice of venue for imbibing, and in the Long Bar can be seen a pair of ship's lanterns, all that remains of the chandlery from Bristol Docks which gave the inn its name. Real ales and an unusual range of country wines are served, and those wishing to partake of lunch or a snack may choose from the good selection of hot and cold dishes, largely home-made, which are available. The Restaurant is open each evening from 7.00 pm for such temptations as whole Dover sole, peppered steak in a cream and brandy sauce, boeuf stroganoff or perhaps roast duckling with orange or cranberries. One singular feature of this charming inn is the orangery or enclosed garden, where one may remain sheltered while enjoying the best of the weather. ♛ ♛ ♛ *Commended, **.*

Berkshire

BIRD IN HAND HOTEL,
Knowl Hill, Twyford, Reading,
Berkshire RG10 9UP

Tel: 062-882 2781/6622

Accommodation (15 bedrooms, all with private bathroom); Free house; Historic interest; Luncheons, dinners and snacks; Car park (90); London 31 miles, Reading 8, Henley-on-Thames 6.

Those who make a point of stopping at this nice little pub to take advantage of the excellent home cooking will be pleased to know that they can now stay a night or two and sample Maura Shone's breakfasts as well. She and Jack had so many people asking for accommodation that they obligingly went ahead and built some, proof that demand does indeed create supply. An extensive hot and cold lunchtime buffet provides something for all tastes, and in addition to the varied à la carte menu, visitors may eat very well indeed at a fixed price. Real ale is served. 🍺🍺🍺🍺, *Michelin, Ashley Courtenay recommended.*

THE SWAN,
East Ilsley, Near Newbury,
Berkshire RG16 0LF

Tel: 063 528 238

Accommodation (10 bedrooms, 8 with private bathroom); Historic interest; Luncheons and dinners (not Sunday evenings or Mondays), snacks; Car park (28); Newbury 9 miles.

A thoroughly delightful inn with its roots in the sixteenth century, the Swan's recent refurbishment has added much in the way of comfort while retaining the atmosphere which enchants visitors old and new. Meals, largely home cooked, are served in both restaurant and open-plan bar, where blackboard specialities supplement the usual menu which includes individual steak and kidney or cottage pies, spicy chilli con carne and wonderfully fragrant steak and onions braised gently in ale. On the subject of ale, a good range is kept and served with friendly good cheer. Guest rooms have en suite facilities, colour television and telephone.

BOULTERS LOCK HOTEL,
Boulters Island, Maidenhead,
Berkshire SL6 8PE

Tel: 0628 21291

Fax: 0628 26048

Accommodation (19 bedrooms, all with private bathroom); Free house; Historic interest; Breakfasts, luncheons, dinners and snacks; Car park (60); London 26 miles, Reading 12.

Originally built at the end of the seventeenth century as a flour mill and cottages, this very special establishment stands on a small island by the loveliest of Thames River locks and is widely known today as one of the area's premier places for a truly memorable cuisine and superior accommodation. Nineteen exquisitely appointed guestrooms provide full en suite facilities, colour television, tea and coffee service, alarm, radio, direct-dial telephone and trouser press, and each has its own individual style and attraction. Single and double rooms are available, as well as mini-suites with views of garden and river (two with their own private terrace), a magnificent four-poster room, and the 'Room at the Top' much favoured by honeymooners, with jacuzzi and comfortable sitting room. Every table in the elaborately decorated restaurant enjoys beautiful river views, but scenery should not be permitted to distract one's attention from the menu, which offers a careful mix of English and Continental cuisine. Service is discreet and unobtrusive, as is the music provided regularly by a resident pianist. If one can bear to leave the charming surroundings of Boulters itself, the hotel's own private launch is the perfect way to see the river.

Buckinghamshire

THE ROYAL STANDARD OF ENGLAND,
Forty Green, Beaconsfield,
Buckinghamshire

Tel: 0494 673382

No accommodation; Free house; Historic interest; Luncheons and snacks; Car park; London 24 miles, Aylesbury 20, Henley-on-Thames 16, High Wycombe 6.

No staff is more willing than that which strives to satisfy the demand for food and drink here. A salient reason for such apparent popularity is the cold buffet which has to be seen to be believed. Choose from 22 cheeses as well as a wide selection of meats and hot dishes. Draught beer and the potent 'Owd Roger' ale can complete a meal to remember. Named by King Charles II, the inn has a fascinating history reflected in its stained glass windows and ancient timbers and is thought to be the oldest free house in the country.

DUNCOMBE ARMS,
32 Lower Way, Great Brickhill,
Milton Keynes, Buckinghamshire MK17 9AG   Tel: 052526 1226

Accommodation (3 bedrooms, all with private shower); Historic interest; Luncheons, dinners and snacks; Car park (14); Aylesbury 12 miles, Dunstable 8, Milton Keynes 4.

Handy for those travelling on the M1, the Duncombe Arms is just four miles from Junction 13 and enjoys a pleasant garden setting overlooking Aylesbury Vale. A choice of table d'hôte and à la carte menus is offered in the charming restaurant, and children are well catered for. Basket meals are available in the bar. Limited accommodation is good value for money, bedrooms are equipped with colour television and teasmade. A particular feature here are the sporting facilities, and patrons can take advantage of the 18-hole putting green, 16 floodlit petanque pitches, American horseshoes, croquet, giant garden chess and garden skittles. *ETB* 👑👑, *AA and RAC Highly Acclaimed.*

ROSE AND CROWN HOTEL,
Saunderton, Near Princes Risborough,
Buckinghamshire HP17 9NP   Tel: 084-44 5299

Accommodation (17 bedrooms, 14 with private bathroom); Free house; Luncheons, dinners and snacks; Car park (60); London 39 miles, Oxford 20, Aylesbury 9.

On the main road (A4010) between Aylesbury and High Wycombe, this attractive Georgian-style free house has facilities that would put many multi-starred hotels in the shade, at the same time retaining its appealing wayside inn atmosphere. A recommended base from which to explore the Chilterns and a lush and gentle countryside, the inn has welcoming bars where traditional ales are sure to be appreciated, and the excellent restaurant operates an interesting menu throughout the week except Sunday evening and Monday lunchtime. The accommodation is of the highest order, guest rooms all having colour television, direct-dial telephone and tea and coffee makers. All rooms have bathrooms en suite.

RED LION,
9 High Street, Wendover,
Buckinghamshire   Tel: 0296 622266

Accommodation (26 bedrooms, all with private bath or shower room); Free house; Historic interest; Dinners and snacks; Car park (50); London 36 miles, Oxford 26.

Rupert Brooke, R.L. Stevenson and Oliver Cromwell number among the distinguished personages to visit this 17th century inn, and although history does not record the opinion of the last-named, the Red Lion would doubtless meet with the Lord Protector's shocked disapproval were he to return today. The sheer comfort of its twenty six freshly decorated bedrooms would be sufficient to offend, without the added self-indulgent wickedness of en suite bath or shower, colour television and tea/coffee making facilities! Those less puritanical in spirit, however, will wallow in the luxury and cosy oak-beamed charm without a twinge of conscience. Good quality bar food is served and an informal restaurant offers a well-priced menu specialising in fish dishes. The bar has a selection of at least four real ales.

CHEQUERS INN,
Wooburn Common, Near Beaconsfield,
Buckinghamshire HP10 0JQ   Tel: 06285 29575 Fax: 0628 850124

*Accommodation (17 bedrooms, all with private bathroom); Free house; Historic interest;
Luncheons, dinners and snacks; Car park (60); London 24 miles, M25 8, Beaconsfield 2.*

It is difficult to know which aspect of this fine old inn to highlight, for it is the careful blend of all
its many charms which makes a stay here such a memorable experience. Only twenty-four
miles from London, Chequers stands sedately at the top of a steep, winding lane in the
undulating Chiltern Hills, and offers magnificent open views of the surrounding countryside.
Guest bedrooms are comfortable and individually styled in a traditional and most pleasing
manner, all seventeen having luxurious private bathroom, remote control colour television,
radio alarm, telephone and beverage-making facilities. Cuisine is French based, but the chef is
at pains to point out that it is not nouvelle cuisine, being intended for hearty appetites and not
just a discerning eye. Pan-fried saddle of venison, well hung game, poultry and the best of
English beef feature temptingly on the well planned menu and a good wine list does justice to
the fare. Chequers' 17th-century tradition of hospitality and hostelry is evident in the quaint
bar presided over by proprietor Peter Roehrig, where gleaming copper and lovingly polished
wood reflect the flames of a winter log fire. *AA**, BTA Commended.*

Cambridgeshire

GEORGE HOTEL,
Great North Road, Buckden,
Cambridgeshire PE18 9XA

Tel: 0480 810307

Accommodation (15 bedrooms, all with private bathroom); Free house; Historic interest; Luncheons, dinners and snacks; Car park; Huntingdon 4 miles.

Legend has it that the notorious highwayman Dick Turpin was a regular visitor to the George, but today's guests are more likely to be weary businessmen in search of rest and refreshment or tourists seeking a cosy base from which to enjoy the attractions of the area. Quality bar meals are available in addition to the exceedingly good-value buffet offered at lunchtime, and evening diners may choose from tempting à la carte and table d'hôte menus. All fifteen en suite guestrooms have tea and coffee facilities, television, radio, hairdryer and telephone and one is furnished with a four-poster bed. Family rooms are available and children made most welcome. *ETB* 👑 👑 👑, ***.

LEEDS ARMS,
2 The Green, Eltisley,
Cambridgeshire PE19 4TG

Tel: 048087 283

Fax: 0480-87 379

Accommodation (9 motel rooms, all with private bathroom); Free house; Luncheons, dinners and snacks; Car park (30); Cambridge 10 miles, St. Neots 6.

Long before community centres were thought of the village hostelry was the place to hear all the news, and a lovely old inn like the Leeds Arms is still the hub of local social life, and well deserves to be. Attractively decorated yet still retaining the old oak beams and an inglenook fireplace with copper hood over a blazing log fire to bring a touch of the old days to modern times, the Leeds Arms offers a range of meals to suit all tastes. There is an extensive bar menu with appetisers, succulent steaks and delicious desserts available all week; also Sunday lunch. Accommodation is of an equally high standard, and rooms are all equipped with colour television, telephone and drinks making facilities. *British Tourist Board Listed.*

FERRY BOAT INN,
Holywell, St. Ives,
Cambridgeshire PE17 3TG

Tel: 0480 63227

Accommodation (7 bedrooms, all with private bathroom); Free house; Historic interest; Luncheons (Sunday), dinners (Saturday evening) and snacks; Car park (50); St. Ives 2 miles.

Part of the granite floor of this ancient inn contains a slab marking the grave of a young woman who committed suicide and was buried here *almost a thousand years ago* — which gives one some idea of the antiquity of the place! The records in fact show that liquor was first retailed here in the year 560, and experts claim that the foundations are a century older still. With all that in mind it somehow comes as a surprise to find such modern wonders as colour television and tea and coffee facilities in the guest accommodation, but travellers may rest assured that comforts are entirely of this century and include en suite bath or shower. It is food, however, as much as accommodation and atmosphere which attracts visitors to the charming, thatched Ferry Boat. Freshest of produce (much of it local), traditional cooking methods and a great deal of loving care combine to produce a cuisine extolled far and wide, the quality of which can be depended upon whether one is choosing a simple bar snack or an elaborate dish from the restaurant's à la carte menu. Only the very best of English ales is served and a lavish selection of wines and spirits make sure that all palates and tastes are catered for. *Egon Ronay.*

RISING SUN INN,
Leverington, Wisbech,
Cambridgeshire PE13 5DH

Tel: 0945 583754

No accommodation; Historic interest; Luncheons, dinners and snacks; Car park (30);
Wisbech 2 miles.

Of considerable antiquity, this lovely old inn is one of the attractive historic features of the delightful village of Leverington along with the 16th century church, 12th century in part, with its tall, decorated spire, a noted landmark for miles around. The inn, with its neat and homely bars, has acquired a wide reputation for its excellent meals, charmingly served, a judgement to which we can emphatically subscribe. Elgoods, the local brewers, supply first-rate ales and for those needing to keep a responsible eye on intake, we can heartily recommend 'Highway', a sparkling beer only one-third the potency of the normal, yet it tastes just as good and is reasonable in price. The inn has the added advantage of a pretty enclosed garden well patronised in fine weather.

THE WHITE HART,
Willingham,
Cambridgeshire

Tel: 0954 60356

No accommodation; Historic interest; Luncheons, dinners and snacks; Car park (40); London 72
miles, Cambridge 9.

When we entered the charming beamed bar on 1st August 1990, controlled pandemonium reigned; Alan and Jenny Butten and family were taking over. Regulars and new-found friends have immediately recognised the expertise of these affable hosts, especially in the field of catering. Alan is noted for his 'Big Al' curries whilst Jenny conjures up delicious pies and flans. One may dine well each weekday and the Sunday lunches offer outstanding value. There is an attractive beer garden and real ale is available. Don't be put off by the occasional glass jumping off the shelf under its own volition — it is only the inn's pet poltergeist and NOT Louise, one of the most efficient (and long suffering!) barmaids it has been our pleasure to meet.

Cheshire

TURNERS ARMS,
Ingersley Road, Bollington,
Near Macclesfield, Cheshire SK10 5RE

Tel: 0625 573864

Accommodation (8 bedrooms, 2 with private facilities); Free house; Historic interest; Luncheons,
dinners and snacks; Macclesfield 3 miles.

Offering all the homely comforts of a traditional northern, family-run inn, the Turners Arms has just eight nicely appointed letting bedrooms, all with colour television, beverage-making facilities and washbasin. A good range of excellent and reasonably priced bar snacks is served in the evenings, and even the splendid à la carte menu available Tuesday to Sunday will not stretch the budget too far. Two of Bollington's old cotton mills still stand, a testament to the town's peak of prosperity in the last century, and there is much of historic and natural interest in the surrounding area. 👑👑

THE PHEASANT INN,
Higher Burwardsley, Tattenhall,
Cheshire CH3 9PF

Tel: 0829 70434

Accommodation (6 bedrooms, all with private bathroom); Free house; Historic interest; Dinners and snacks; Car park (60); Tarporley 5 miles.

For 300 years the lovely half timbered and sandstone Pheasant Inn has stood atop the Peckforton Hills, gazing out over the Cheshire Plain to distant Wales. Panoramic views are to be enjoyed from all the nicely decorated bedrooms, which are complete with en suite bathroom, colour television, radio alarm, hairdryer and beverage making facilities. Accommodation is in the beautifully converted barn, tucked quietly away from the convivial bar with its huge log fire, and the Bistro Restaurant which enjoys a well-deserved reputation for fine fare, well presented and served with cheerful efficiency. Weekend mini-breaks are a popular feature of this commendable establishment.

OLD HALL HOTEL,
Newcastle Road, Sandbach,
Cheshire CW11 0AL

Tel: 0270 761221
Fax: 0270 762551

Accommodation (15 bedrooms, all with private bathroom); Free house; Historic interest; Luncheons, dinners and snacks; Car park (50); Stoke-on-Trent 13 miles, Middlewich 5.

As gracious and stately as its name suggests, this seventeenth-century, black and white timbered hotel stands amid well-kept gardens on the edge of Sandbach, just a mile from the M6 motorway. Recently refurbished guest accommodation includes single, twin and double rooms all of which have bath or shower en suite and the facilities of colour television, telephone, tea and coffee tray, trouser press and hairdryer. Meals and snacks are served in the bar each lunchtime except Sunday, and full à la carte and table d'hôte menus are offered in the Jacobean Restaurant open Monday to Saturday evening and for Sunday lunch. ♚♚♚♚ *Commended, ***.*

SUTTON HALL,
Bullocks Lane, Sutton, Macclesfield,
Cheshire SK11 0HE

Tel: 02605 3211

Fax: 02605 2538

Accommodation (10 bedrooms, all with private bathroom); Free house; Historic interest;
Luncheons, dinners and snacks; Car park; Stockport 10 miles.

One hesitates to describe this one-time baronial residence and former convent as an *inn* —
and yet in its virtues of good ale, good food and good rest it ably carries on all the best
traditions of innkeeping in addition to supplying country house elegance and not a little
luxury. Each of the ten guest bedrooms is furnished with an elaborately draped fourposter bed
and is appointed to the highest standard with colour television, tea and coffee facilities and
bathroom en suite. Cuisine is on a par with accommodation, and a comprehensive range of
good bar food is available as well as the more formal fare of the dining room. 🏆🏆🏆

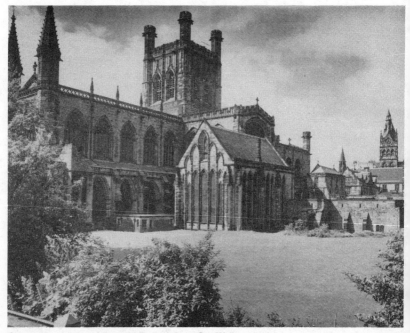

Chester Cathedral and Town Hall tower from City Walls.

Cornwall

OLD FERRY INN,
Bodinnick-by-Fowey,
Cornwall PL23 1LY

Tel: 0726 870237

Accommodation (12 bedrooms, 7 with private bathroom); Free house; Historic interest; Bar Lunches, dinners and snacks; Car park (8); Liskeard 15 miles, Looe 10.

Under the supervision of Mr and Mrs S.A. Farr, this 400-year-old hostelry, fully licensed, combines the charm of a past era with modern comfort. Rooms are well-appointed, and several bedrooms have private bathrooms. A reputation has been rapidly gained for fine food and wine. This free house stands in a quiet sheltered position facing south, overlooking the beautiful Fowey estuary. Bodinnick is a splendid centre for sailing, boating and fishing; Fowey, easily reached by car ferry, has a famous yachting harbour. There are lovely coastal walks in the vicinity. *British Tourist Authority Commended Country Hotel.*

TRENGILLY WARTHA INN,
Nancenoy, Constantine, Near Falmouth,
Cornwall TR11 5RP

Tel: 0326 40332

Accommodation (6 bedrooms, 5 with private bathroom); Free house; Dinners and snacks; Car park (50); Helston 7 miles, Falmouth 6.

Whatever season one chooses to visit this family-run free house, one is sure of being charmed, whether by its well-kept garden and delightful views in summer, or the cosiness of the bar with its wood-burning fires when the winds blow chilly outside. Even on the coldest day guests will find their pretty bedrooms snug and comfortable, all being centrally heated. Colour television, direct-dial telephone and beverage-makers are provided. A fixed price menu is presented in the restaurant, and satisfying bar meals are available every lunchtime and evening, complemented by an extensive wine list and real ales.

PUNCH BOWL INN,
Lanreath, Near Looe,
Cornwall PL13 2NX

Tel: 0503 20218

Accommodation (14 bedrooms, 11 with private bathroom); Free house; Historic interest; Luncheons (Sundays), dinners and snacks; Car park (60); Looe 5 miles.

There is something infinitely solid and enduring about this old hostelry, as if it could withstand the sun, rain and wind of the next four hundred years as uncomplainingly as it has withstood the ravages of the past four centuries. In turn courthouse, coaching inn and smugglers' distribution house, it now serves as a peaceful hideaway for visitors to this charmed corner of the world. Bedrooms in both modern and traditional style are available, all with colour television and tea and coffee facilities, and some with private bath or shower, and the first rate cuisine features many Cornish specialities well worth sampling. *AA and RAC**, Ashley Courtenay, Egon Ronay.*

ROYAL OAK,
Duke Street, Lostwithiel,
Cornwall PL22 1AH

Tel: 0208 872552

Accommodation (6 bedrooms, all with private bathroom); Free house; Historic interest; Dinners and snacks; Car park; Liskeard 11 miles, Fowey 7.

As full of character as the village in which it is situated, the thirteenth-century Royal Oak is tucked away just off the main road and has an underground tunnel said to connect its cellar to the dungeons of Restormel Castle, providing a smuggling route and possibly an escape route. Today one can escape to the hostelry via the A390, and once there will find two beautifully kept bars, one of which does duty as a restaurant where good à la carte meals are served nightly. Overnight guests are accommodated in nicely furnished en suite bedrooms with television, radio and tea-making facilities. *RAC 2 Tankards.*

THE WHITE HART,
Menheniot, Liskeard,
Cornwall

Tel: 0579 42245/47648

Accommodation (6 bedrooms, all with private bathroom or shower); Free house; Historic interest; Luncheons, dinners and snacks; Car park (40); Plymouth 15 miles, Looe 8, Liskeard 3.

This busy village inn enjoys charming and peaceful surroundings, yet historic Plymouth and fascinating Looe may be easily reached. The accommodation available at this friendly retreat is of a high order indeed, all guest rooms having private bath facilities, as well as colour television, telephone, and tea and coffee making facilities. Satisfying à la carte meals are served, whilst snacks are always obtainable in any of the three bars. Dating back to the seventeenth century, this old hostelry is well recommended as a peaceful holiday venue, the atmosphere encouraged by open log fires and beams, in addition to convivial company.

JUBILEE INN,
Pelynt, Near Looe,
Cornwall PL13 2JZ

Tel: 0503 20312

Accommodation (12 bedrooms, all with private bathroom); Free house; Historic interest; Luncheons, dinners and snacks; Car park; Launceston 25 miles, Bodmin 16, Fowey (ferry) 5, Looe 4.

The old world is preserved to a very high standard in this comfortable and spacious Wayside Inn. This 400-year-old inn, situated on the Looe-Lostwithiel road is attractively furnished throughout has en suite rooms with colour TV, is centrally heated, with log fires in winter. The village of Pelynt is conveniently situated two miles from the sea. Excellent for sailing, boating, bathing and fishing. Covered car spaces and large car park, as well as attractive gardens and lawns with safe children's play area — ideal for parents relaxing with a drink or snack. An evening barbecue, under cover if necessary, is a weekly feature in high season. *ETB* 👑 👑 👑, *AA and RAC ***.

THE WEARY FRIAR,
Pillaton, Saltash,
Cornwall PL12 6QS

Tel: 0579 50238

Accommodation (14 bedrooms, all with private bathroom); Free house; Historic interest; Luncheons, dinners and snacks; Car park (60); London 218 miles, Launceston 14, Looe 13, Liskeard 11, Plymouth 8, Saltash 6.

This twelfth-century country hotel of character is set in beautiful surroundings, and is famous for good food and real ales from a well-stocked bar, in an atmosphere of traditional comfort. All the bedrooms are en suite, with colour television and tea-making facilities. This is an excellent touring centre, being only two and a half miles from St. Mellion Golf Course, with riding and fishing available locally. Bar meals are served lunchtimes and evenings, and there is an extensive à la carte menu available in the restaurant in the evening.

DRIFTWOOD SPARS HOTEL,
Trevaunance Cove, St. Agnes,
Cornwall TR5 0RT

Tel: 087-255 2428/3323

Accommodation (11 rooms, many with private facilities); Free house; Historic interest; Luncheons, snacks, dinners; Large car park; Newquay 12 miles, Truro 8, Redruth 7.

Situated only a hundred yards from the beach, the building which is now the popular Driftwood Spars Hotel is over 300 years old and has seen active service as a tin miner's store, a chandlery, a sailmaker's workshop and a fish cellar. But nowadays, the emphasis is strictly on providing guests with good food, ale and atmosphere. There are three bars — one has a children's room — serving a selection of real ales, including a weekly guest beer, and appetising home cooked food. Delicious candlelit dinners, featuring fresh local seafood, game and steaks, can be enjoyed in the new à la carte restaurant. Driftwood Spars offers 11 bedrooms, most with private facilities, colour television, telephone, tea-making equipment and sea views. Please telephone or write for brochure.

CROWN INN,
St. Ewe, Near Mevagissey,
Cornwall PL26 6EY

Tel: 0726 843322

Accommodation (3 bedrooms); Historic interest; Luncheons, dinners and snacks; Car park; St Austell 5 miles, Mevagissey 3.

This is a nice, unassuming old inn which one might easily pass on the road from St Austell to Mevagissey, but the unfortunates who fail to notice it miss a rare treat. Excellent homemade food is served in a rather quaint dining room small enough to preserve an intimate atmosphere, and the well-stocked bar retains the flagstone floor and heavy beams of the 1500s. Simple but beautifully kept overnight accommodation is provided in three letting bedrooms, and a hearty breakfast is included in the very modest charge. Proprietors Norman and Ruth Jeffery are as charming as their establishment, and offer every assistance to the visitor.

WHITE HART,
St. Teath,
Cornwall

Tel: 0208 850281

Accommodation (2 bedrooms); Free house; Historic interest; Luncheons, dinners and snacks; Car park (150); Camelford 3 miles.

Very much the village inn, this friendly free house is as popular with locals as it is with visitors to the area, always a good recommendation of any hostelry. Bar food which is served both lunchtime and evening ranges from the simple sandwich to good, modestly priced steaks, and service is as cheerful and warming as the coal fire which burns on chillier days. Those seeking accommodation in the village will find spotlessly clean, well furnished guest rooms at the White Hart, and a full Cornish breakfast is included in the most reasonable charge. Children are made very welcome.

MILLHOUSE INN,
Trebarwith, Tintagel,
Cornwall PL34 0HD

Tel: 0840 770200

Accommodation (9 bedrooms, all with private bathroom); Free house; Historic interest; Dinners and snacks; Car park (40); Barnstaple 54 miles, Launceston 20, Wadebridge 16.

As snug as a Cornish cat in its wooded valley, this former flour mill is just a few minutes' walk from the beach and cliffs at Trebarwick Strand, and conveniently situated for touring all of this charmed county. Country-cottage bedrooms provide a home-from-home, each having private bath or shower and WC, tea and coffee facilities, colour television, radio and hairdryer. Heavy beams and flagstone floors lend character to the busy main bar where tasty food is served lunchtime and evening, and the Terrace Bar leads onto the Restaurant, where evening dinner proves a memorable and most satisfying experience.

Cumbria

TUFTON ARMS HOTEL,
Market Square, Appleby-in-Westmorland, Cumbria CA16 6XA

Tel: 07683 51593
Fax: 07683 52761

Accommodation (19 bedrooms, all with private bathroom); Free house; Historic interest; Luncheons, dinners and snacks; Kendal 24 miles, Penrith 13.

When the Milsom family took over this late sixteenth-century inn, they commissioned interior designer Barbara Brocklebank to help them restore it to the splendour of its Victorian heyday, and her ample talents are displayed throughout the fine building. Nineteen bedrooms provide a range of accommodation in varying styles and standards, with three well-appointed suites, three superior doubles, six 'ordinary' doubles and eight singles. All have the facilities of colour television, video, radio, tea tray and direct-dial telephone, and those overlooking the quaint market place are double glazed to ensure that outside activities do not disturb. Dinner at the Tufton Arms is something of an experience, and the elegant Conservatory Restaurant is a most worthy setting for the finest of cuisine prepared by head chef David Milsom and his dedicated helpers. Only the finest quality fresh produce is used and each dish, specially cooked to order, will find its perfect partner on the extensive wine list. After the meal one might care to take coffee and liqueurs in the beautifully furnished drawing room, or perhaps adjourn to the bar to meet and mingle with the locals. An open fire warms this room when the winds blow chilly, and meals and snacks are provided lunchtime and early evening. *ETB* 👑 👑 👑 👑, *RAC* ***.

THE PUNCH BOWL,
Askham, Penrith, Cumbria CA10 2PF

Tel: 09312 443

Accommodation (4 bedrooms); Historic interest; Luncheons, dinners and snacks; Car park; Penrith 4 miles.

The strains and stresses of city life are soon forgotten at this 17th century Cumbrian inn, situated in the unspoilt village of Askham at the western side of the aptly named Eden Valley. A hearty English breakfast is included in the modest charge for overnight accommodation here and guestrooms are spacious, well decorated and furnished with thought to comfort. Family rooms are available. Varied homecooked fare is offered, with delicious pies a tribute to the Swiss-trained chef whose hands have fashioned them, and packed lunches are readily provided for day outings. Log fires and oak beams give atmosphere to a locally popular bar whee good conversation may be shared. This is an ideal base for touring the Lake District.

DRUNKEN DUCK INN,
Barngates, Ambleside,
Cumbria LA22 0NG

Tel: 09666 347

Accommodation (10 bedrooms, all with private bathroom); Free house; Historic interest; Snacks; Car park (40); Windermere 4 miles.

This unique establishment has been dispensing hospitality and cheer for over four hundred years, but its present name was acquired less than a century ago when a barrel on stillage in the cellar slipped its hoops and the contents seeped into the ducks' feeding ditch. Thus was born the name which is as memorable and unusual as the inn itself. Set in sixty acres of enchanting Cumbrian scenery, accommodation here comprises ten individually designed guestrooms furnished in traditional style with antiques, tester beds and patchwork quilts, but with such modern conveniences as colour television, beverage-making facilities, hairdryer and of course private bathroom. Food is plentiful, varied and beautifully cooked, and old Lakeland favourites like Cumberland sausage casserole or Leek, Bacon and Butterbean Bake will delight the most jaded of tastebuds. Hearty old-fashioned puddings such as spotted dick and roly poly are a speciality too — though how diners cope with them on a day which has begun with the Duck's "Compleat Breakfast" is a mystery indeed! Half-price fishing tickets are available to residents who wish to use the inn's well-stocked tarn, and there is also private shooting. Although seemingly isolated, all the varied pleasures of Lakeland are but a short drive away. *ETB* 🏆 🏆 🏆, *AA, Ashley Courtenay recommended.*

HARE AND HOUNDS INN,
Bowland Bridge, Grange-over-Sands,
Cumbria
Tel: 04488 333 (reception) 04488 777 (guests)

Accommodation (16 bedroooms, most with private bathroom); Free house; Historic interest; Luncheons, dinners and snacks; Car park (80); Grange-over-Sands 9 miles, Kendal 8, Windermere 7.

With a tranquil situation in the beautiful Winster Valley and yet conveniently near to the popular pleasures of Windermere, the Hare and Hounds is a delightful residential hostelry with a warm welcome for all. All bedrooms have a telephone, and there is a comfortable lounge. The lounge bar with its oak beams, stone walls and log fires has a typical Lakeland atmosphere, and meals are served at midday and in the evening. There is a beer garden and, isolated by the rolling Cartmel Fells, the inn which dates from 1600 is conveniently placed for numerous beauty spots and places of historic interest. Terms for overnight accommodation represent good value, and special bargain breaks in winter are organised. Access and Visa welcome. *ETB* 👑 👑 👑, *Egon Ronay Recommended.*

The Coledale Inn

COLEDALE INN,
Braithwaite, Near Keswick,
Cumbria CA12 5TN
Tel: 059-682 272

Accommodation (8 bedrooms, all with private shower/WC); Free house; Luncheons, dinners and snacks; Car park (16); Carlisle 30 miles, Cockermouth 10, Keswick 2.

A friendly, family run Victorian Inn in a peaceful hillside position above Braithwaite, and ideally situated for touring and walking, with paths to the mountains immediately outside our gardens. All bedrooms are warm and spacious, with en suite shower room and colour television. Children are welcome. Home cooked meals are served every lunchtime and evening, with a fine selection of inexpensive wines, beers and Coledale XXPS real cask ale. Open all year except midweek lunches in winter. Tariff and menu sent on request. 👑 👑 👑 👑

COTTAGE IN THE WOOD,
Whinlatter Pass, Braithwaite,
Keswick, Cumbria CA12 5TW

Tel: 059-682 409

Accommodation (7 bedrooms, all en-suite); Historic interest; Morning coffee, afternoon teas and snacks; Car park (20); Cockermouth 8 miles, Buttermere 8, Keswick 4.

A charming seventeenth century former coaching inn beautifully and remotely situated atop Whinlatter Pass in the heart of Thornthwaite Forest, and offering the very best of Lakeland hospitality. A freshly prepared, thoughtfully planned five-course meal is served each evening. Relax afterwards with coffee in the comfortable lounge, where on colder evenings a log fire burns brightly. All bedrooms are en suite, with hot drinks facilities and central heating; two have four-poster beds. Pets strictly by prior arrangement only. Resident owners Sandra and Barrie Littlefair look forward to giving all their guests a warm welcome. *ETB* 👑 👑 👑 *Commended.*

THE BLACKSMITH'S ARMS,
Talkin Village, Brampton,
Cumbria CA8 1LE

Tel: 06977 3452

Accommodation (5 bedrooms, all with private bathroom); Free house; Historic interest; Dinners and snacks; Car park (30); Newcastle-upon-Tyne 66 miles, Carlisle 9, Brampton 1.

The Blacksmith's Arms offers all the hospitality and comforts of a traditional country inn. Enjoy tasty meals served in the bar lounges, or linger over dinner in the well-appointed restaurant. The inn is personally managed by the proprietors Pat and Tom Bagshaw, who guarantee the hospitality one would expect from a family concern. Guests are assured of a pleasant and comfortable stay. There are five lovely bedrooms, all en suite and offering every comfort. Peacefully situated in the beautiful village of Talkin, the inn is convenient for the Borders, Hadrian's Wall and the Lake District. There is a good golf course, pony trekking, walking and other country pursuits nearby. *FHG Best Bed and Breakfast Diploma Winners 1989.*

CONISTON SUN HOTEL,
Coniston,
Cumbria LA21 8HQ

Tel: 05394 41248

Accommodation (11 bedrooms, all with private bathroom); Free house; Historic interest; Dinners and snacks; Car park (20); Kendal 21 miles, Windermere 13, Ambleside 8.

Huddled in the shelter of Coniston Old Man and just a mile from Coniston Water, this traditional Cumbrian inn was Donald Campbell's base while attempting the world water speed record. Those who prefer life at a more leisurely pace, however, will be charmed by its tranquil atmosphere and air of old world graciousness. Two of the eleven guestrooms have four-poster beds, and all are equipped with colour television, beverage-making facilities and bathroom en suite. Central heating and log fires ensure year-round comfort and make this a cosy choice for an out-of-season break. Food is good and beautifully presented.

WHOOP HALL INN,
Burrow-with-Burrow, Kirkby Lonsdale,
Carnforth, Lancashire LA6 2HP
Tel: 05242 71284

Accommodation (17 luxury bedrooms, all with private bathroom); Free house; Historic interest; Luncheons, dinners and snacks; Car parking; M6 (Junction 36) 6 miles.

While booking in advance is recommended at the Whoop Hall's deservedly popular Gallery Restaurant, a less formal meal can be obtained at the Buttery. As well as traditional English fare, the menu here features a good choice of pasta dishes, with several kinds of lasagne and delicious creamed noodles with ham and cheese. Bedrooms are in country cottage style, all en suite and with colour television and beverage making facilities, and a particularly charming four-poster room is available, complete with jacuzzi bath. If the lucky people who secure it can tear themselves away, they will find the inn extremely well placed for touring both Lakes and Dales. *ETB* ♛ ♛ ♛ ♛ *Commended, AA and RAC **.*

BRITANNIA INN,
Elterwater, Near Ambleside,
Cumbria LA22 9HP
Tel: 096-67 210/382 or (1991/92) 05394 37210/37382

Accommodation (9 bedrooms, 6 with private facilities); Free house; Historic interest; Luncheons, dinners and snacks; Car park; London 270 miles, Coniston 5, Ambleside 4, Grasmere 3.

A genuine old-world, 400-year-old inn overlooking the village green in the delightful unspoilt village of Elterwater in the beautiful Langdale Valley. The inn is renowned for its fine food and excellent wine cellar, and is also open to non-residents for dinner in the evening. There are seven double bedrooms, five of which have en suite shower and toilet; two twin-bedded rooms, one of which has shower and toilet. All are newly furnished and have tea and coffee making facilities, hair driers, colour television and central heating. With open fires burning cheerfully in the bars, the inn has a lively atmosphere, and is a popular venue by reason of its bar meals, menu and choice of traditional ales. A warm welcome is assured by the resident proprietor, David Fry and his staff. For motorists there is parking, and facilities nearby include fishing, sailing, fell walking, pony trekking and hound trails. The inn is closed at Christmas.

KINGS ARMS,
The Square, Hawkshead, Ambleside,
Cumbria LA22 0NZ

Tel: 09666 372

Accommodation (10 bedrooms, 6 with private bathroom); Free house; Historic interest; Dinners and snacks; Ambleside 4 miles.

The old Kings Arms looks over the Square of this charming Lakeland village, where little seems to have changed since the days when Wordsworth attended the local grammar school and lodged at Anne Tyson's cottage. Oak beams and open fire grace the cosy bar, where the real ale is served and a nice range of snacks may be enjoyed lunchtime and evening. Those wishing more formal dining are directed to the excellent restaurant, where an extensive wine list complements the à la carte menu. Guestrooms are well furnished, with colour television and beverage facilities, and additional accommodation is available in attractive Fern Cottage, just a step from the hotel itself.

THE WOOLPACK INN,
Holmrook, Boot,
Cumbria CA19 1TH

Tel: 094-03 230

Accommodation (7 bedrooms, 4 with private shower); Free house; Historic interest; Dinners and snacks; Whitehaven 15 miles.

Dating back to the seventeenth century, this lovely old Cumbrian inn is situated at the head of the picturesque Eskdale Valley, about one mile from the foot of Hardknott Pass. The scenery here of course is some of the most beautiful and impressive in the Lakes, and the Woolpack is well placed for both fell walkers and those who prefer to tour by car. Ample and appetising home-cooked meals await your return, and the Fox family will do their utmost to make your stay pleasant and relaxing in this warm and friendly inn.

KIRKSTILE INN,
Loweswater, Cockermouth,
Cumbria CA13 0RU

Tel: 090-085 219

Accommodation (10 bedrooms, 8 with private bathroom); Free house; Historic interest; Luncheons, dinners and snacks; Car park; Workington 12 miles, Keswick 11, Cockermouth 8.

This delightful sixteenth century inn offers good food, friendly service and real ale in a traditional setting of low-beamed rooms and open fires. Most bedrooms have private bathrooms; all have extensive views of the surrounding fells, excellent for walking and climbing. Nearby are facilities for fishing, boating, golf and tennis.

THE MILL INN,
Mungrisdale, Penrith,
Cumbria CA11 0XR

Tel: 059-683 632

Accommodation (7 bedrooms, 4 with private bath/shower room); Free house; Historic interest; Luncheons, dinners and snacks; Car park (20); Keswick 10 miles, Ullswater 6.

Echoes of colourful days gone by, when characters such as the famous Cumbrian huntsman John Peel used to gather at this fine sixteenth century inn, still linger amongst its stout stone walls. Now that it is once again a free house under the care of resident proprietors, after many years as a tied house, its excellent cask conditioned real ale will awaken more immediate memories of the "good old days"! The inn has now been fully renovated. Indeed, good old-fashioned hospitality is a feature of the Mill Inn, together with a genuine warm welcome, excellent bar meals, and comfortable accommodation (with five-course dinners and full English breakfast for residents). A superb situation in a quiet village close to the foot of Blencathra and the Skiddaw range of fells on the banks of the River Glendermackin make it a welcome retreat from crowded Lakeland resorts. *ETB* 🏵️ 🏵️, *AA, RAC, Derek Johansen, Les Routiers.*

Publisher's Note

When you are booking ahead, please ask for written confirmation, including price and whatever else is included. If you have to cancel, give as long written notice as possible. Your booking is a form of contract and both the proprietor and yourself have obligations as a result.

It is important that you raise any complaints on the spot. In the unlikely event of a serious complaint not being settled to your satisfaction, you should let us know and we will follow it up. We cannot accept responsibility for the details of the published descriptions or for errors or omissions, but we are obviously anxious that you should enjoy whatever use you make of our entries and that the high standards are maintained.

GEORGE HOTEL,
Devonshire Street, Penrith, Cumbria CA11 7SU

Tel: 0768 62696
Fax: 0768 68223

Accommodation (30 bedrooms); Free house; Historic interest; Luncheons, dinners and snacks; Car park (30); Kendal 25 miles, Ambleside 22, Carlisle 18, Keswick 16.

Prince Charles Edward Stuart is believed to number amongst the former guests of this 300-year-old coaching inn, centrally situated in the bustling market town of Penrith and just five miles from Ullswater. Copper and brass, old prints and antique furniture add character to the oak-beamed lounges where today's visitors may relax and enjoy service which is friendly while being courteous and quietly efficient. Imaginative fare is beautifully presented in the restaurant, and in the lounge bar savoury snacks and a tempting cold buffet are available each day except Sunday. All en suite guestrooms have tea-making facilities, colour television, radio and telephone, and out-of-season breaks are good value for money.

THE BLACK SWAN HOTEL,
Ravendale, Kirkby Stephen, Cumbria CA17 4NG

Tel: 05873 204

Accommodation (20 bedrooms, 18 with private bathroom); Free house; Luncheons, dinners and snacks; Car park (28); Kendal 25 miles.

The Black Swan Hotel is a family-run, stone-built inn in the centre of the peaceful Ravenstonedale village. All bedrooms have television and telephone. The hotel enjoys an excellent reputation for cuisine, and has private fishing rights on the rivers Eden and Lune. Other outdoor pursuits include fell walking, bowling green and hard tennis court. Situated seven minutes from M6 Junction 38 and thirty minutes from the Lakes. *ETB Commended, AA, RAC **, Egon Ronay, Ashley Courtenay.*

HARE AND HOUNDS INN,
Talkin Village, Near Brampton, Cumbria CA8 1LE

Tel: 06977 3456/7

Accommodation (4 bedrooms, 2 with private bathroom); Free house; Historic interest; Snacks; Car park (12); Brampton 3 miles.

Once frequented by monks on their way to Lanercost Priory, this attractive and welcoming country inn is run by Pauline and John Goddard, an amicable couple who do everything in their power to ensure that guests' requirements are met in full, whether these be for overnight accommodation or simply a quick meal and refreshment. Atmosphere is pleasant and hospitable with open fires and soft lighting, and bedrooms are comfortably furnished, one with a four-poster bed. A full English breakfast is included in reasonable room charge, and the excellent bar menu ranges from soups and baked potatoes to fillet steaks and good home-made specials.

WILSON ARMS,
Torver, Near Coniston,
Cumbria LA21 8BB

Tel: 05394 41237

Accommodation (7 bedrooms, 4 with private bathroom); Free house; Luncheons, dinners and snacks; Car park (30); Coniston 2 miles.

This friendly guest house and inn is situated in the beautiful Lake District, within easy reach of Coniston Water and the central Lakes. This is an ideal walking area, with miles of unspoilt countryside and many fascinating little villages to explore. The Wilson Arms makes a perfect base at any time of year, with the welcome prospect of a delicious home-cooked meal and a cosy log fire at the end of the day. Fishing and riding are also available in the area. The comfortable rooms have television and tea/coffee making facilities. Special terms for weekend breaks apply during November, December and January, excluding Christmas and New Year. *Les Routiers.*

QUEENS ARMS INN AND MOTEL,
Warwick-on-Eden, Carlisle,
Cumbria CA4 8PA

Tel: 0228 60699

Accommodation (9 bedrooms, all with private bathroom); Free house; Dinners and snacks; Car park (80); Carlisle 4 miles.

On arrival at the Queens Arms one finds in one's room biscuits, tea-making facilities and television — a small point, perhaps, with which to begin a description of so excellent an establishment, but a good indication of the careful attention to detail that is found throughout this sixteenth century inn. Great log fires burn in the original farmhouse fireplaces, while the decor is in that apparently "cluttered and casual manner" not always easy to achieve with good results. Service is warm and friendly — yet always courteous. Everything seems so cheerful and effortless that one can happily forget the hard work necessary to create such an impression. In the restaurant guests may sample exciting and delicious fare; bar food is also available. In warmer weather, meals can be served in the beer garden, where your children can play in the playground while you relax in the sun.

WASDALE HEAD INN,
Wasdale Head, Near Gosforth,
Cumbria CA20 1EX

Tel: 09467 26229

Accommodation (11 bedrooms, all with private bathrooms); 2 self-catering flats and a cottage); Free house; Historic interest; Car park (50); Whitehaven 21 miles.

Splendidly isolated on the fells near Wastwater, and well off the tourist track, this fine old inn embodies something of the spirit of adventure that attracted early climbers and tourists to this remote part of the Lakes. Panelled walls, cushioned settles, and a comfortable old-fashioned atmosphere prove a perfect antidote to the more commercialised and noisy hostelries of the popular resorts. Real ale and home-made bar food will satisfy the sturdiest fresh-air appetites, and the superb five-course dinner menu is excellent value for money. *ETB* 🦀 🦀 🦀 🦀, *AA and RAC **.*

BAY HORSE INN,
Winton, Near Kirkby Stephen,
Cumbria CA17 4HS

Tel: 076-83 71451

Accommodation (3 bedrooms, all with private bathroom); Free house; Historic interest; Dinners and snacks; Car park (6); M6 (Junction 38) 11 miles, Appleby 10, Brough 3, Kirkby Stephen 1.

A warm and welcoming little inn situated on the western side of the scenic Cumbrian Pennines, and ideally placed as a stopping-off point on your journey north or south on the nearby M6. Resident proprietors Sheila and Derek Parvin offer the warmest of welcomes to all guests, with the finest of traditional ales, good food and comfortable accommodation. Lying as it does in the picturesque Eden Valley, the Bay Horse is also ideal as a touring base for those wishing to stay longer in this lovely part of the country. Open all year.

Derbyshire

YE DERWENT HOTEL,
Bamford, Near Sheffield,
Derbyshire S30 2AY

Tel: 0433 51395

Accommodation (10 bedrooms, one with private bathroom, one with private shower); Free house; Luncheons and dinners; Car park (40); Bakewell 17 miles, Sheffield 13.

For those tempted to linger awhile in this lovely "Jane Eyre" country, Angela and David Ryan invite you to Ye Derwent Hotel, which provides comfortable accommodation and a friendly welcome. A full meal service is available in the pleasant dining room, and darts, dominoes, cribbage, backgammon and shove ha'penny can be played in the cosy bar, while enjoying a pint of real ale. Fishing is available nearby. This is an ideal base for exploring the dales and moors.

THE SNAKE PASS INN,
Ashopton Woodlands, Bamford,
Derbyshire S30 2BJ

Tel: 0433 51480

Licensed; All bedrooms with private bathrooms; Children welcome; Car park; Bamford 8 miles, Glossop 7.

Situated in the beautiful Ashopton Woodlands and on the A57 Snake Pass road from Manchester to Sheffield, the Snake Pass Inn is an ideal centre for walkers and ramblers. The Peak District National Park is criss-crossed by numerous footpaths, and the Inn is convenient for many of them. Set in its own grounds with ample car parking, the hotel offers accommodation in single or double rooms, each with en suite bathroom and tea/coffee making facilities. Attached to the hotel is a 15-sleeper camping barn offering low cost alternative accommodation.

YE OLDE CHESHIRE CHEESE,
How Lane, Castleton,
Derbyshire S30 2WJ

Tel: 0433 20330

Accommodation (6 bedrooms, all with private bathroom); Free house; Dinners and snacks; Car park (100); Manchester 17 miles, Sheffield 17.

The "Cheshire Cheese Inn" is a delightful 17th century free house situated in Castleton, Derbyshire – the heart of the Peak District National Park. It is an ideal base for walkers and climbers, with other sporting activities in the area including cycling, golf, swimming, gliding, hang gliding, horse riding and fishing. Castleton itself holds many a treat in store, with its caves and mines, including the world famous "Blue John" mine. There are six pretty bedrooms with colour TV and en suite facilities. Our "Village Fayre" menu is available lunchtimes and evenings, all dishes home cooked in traditional manner – pies, lasagne, chilli etc. Daily specials include roast wild boar, smoked chicken and roast hock. Game menu in winter. No juke box, no pool, no machines, just a traditional 17th century inn. Full Fire Certificate.

CHEQUERS INN,
Froggatt Edge, Near Sheffield,
Derbyshire S30 1ZB

Tel: 0433 30231

Accommodation (3 bedrooms); Historic interest; Snacks (not Sunday evenings); Car park; Baslow 3 miles.

Comfortably furnished guest bedrooms with fresh decor, colour television and facilities for making tea and coffee stand ready for those seeking accommodation at this attractively situated inn, which is run by Ian and Jill McLeod and is old-fashioned in the *nicest* possible sense. Hot and cold bar snacks are offered from noon till 2.00 pm each day and from 6.00 until 9.00 Monday to Saturday evenings, and traditional Sunday lunch is served. Patrons with children will be pleased to note that there is a family room, and that a children's menu is available. 👑👑

BOATHOUSE INN,
Matlock Dale, Matlock,
Derbyshire
Tel: 0629 583776

Accommodation (3 bedrooms); Historic interest; Luncheons, dinners and snacks; Car park; Nottingham 24 miles, Buxton 20, Derby 18, Ashbourne 13, Chesterfield 10.

With comfortable bedrooms overlooking the River Derwent this is, indeed, a pleasant place in which to stay. It is an ideal base from which to explore an area of great beauty yet shops are near at hand. Fine meals are served in the quaint bars with the enjoyment heightened, perhaps, with a jug of real ale.

LATHKIL HOTEL,
Over Haddon, Near Bakewell,
Derbyshire DE4 1JE
Tel: 0629 812501

Accommodation (4 bedrooms, all with private bathroom); Free house; Dinners and snacks; Car park (28); Ashbourne 19 miles, Sheffield 16, Matlock 8.

Those who expect blaring juke boxes and fruit machines will be sadly disappointed in this extra-special establishment, for such modern irritants are very much frowned upon. Here all is as tranquil and relaxing as the surrounding countryside, providing a perfect haven in which to forget the pressure of the workaday world. Colour television, en suite bath or shower, clock radio, personal bar and tea-making facilities are standard in all bedrooms, pleasingly furnished and limited in number to ensure personal attention to each cherished guest. A well stocked hot and cold buffet table supplies ample lunchtime sustenance daily and a fine à la carte menu is offered in the restaurant at night.

PEACOCK HOTEL,
Rowsley, Near Matlock,
Derbyshire DE4 2EB
Tel: 0629 733518/9
Fax: 0629 732671

Accommodation (20 bedrooms, 15 with private bathroom); Historic interest; Breakfast, luncheons, dinners and snacks; Car park (45); Bakewell 3 miles.

Built in the days when wolves roamed the beautiful Peak District, this fine old manor house on the banks of the River Derwent has been offering a retreat to weary travellers for more than half of its long life. Today guests are accommodated both in the hotel itself and in the pleasant cottage annexe, and all comfortable, well-furnished bedrooms are equipped with colour television, beverage-making facilities, radio and telephone. Most have private bath or shower. Excellent luncheon and dinner menus are presented in the attractive restaurant and a good buffet lunch is set out in the lounge Monday to Saturday. Trout fishing on the Rivers Wye and Derwent is available to residents. 👑 👑 👑 👑, *AA and RAC****.

THE DOG AND PARTRIDGE COUNTRY INN,
Swinscoe, Ashbourne,
Derbyshire DE6 2HS

Tel: 0335 43183 Fax: 0335 42742

Accommodation (29 bedrooms, all with private bathroom); Free house; Historic interest; Luncheons, dinners and snacks; Car park (100); Ashbourne 3 miles.

Mary and Martin Stelfox welcome you to a family-run seventeenth century inn and motel set in five acres, five miles from Alton Towers and close to Dovedale and Ashbourne. We specialise in family breaks, and special diets and vegetarians are catered for. All rooms have private bathrooms, colour television, direct-dial telephone, tea-making facilities and baby listening service. It is ideally situated for touring Stoke Potteries, Derbyshire Dales and Staffordshire moorlands. The restaurant is open all day, and non-residents are welcome. 👑👑👑👑.

GEORGE HOTEL,
Tideswell,
Derbyshire

Tel: 0298 871382

Accommodation (4 bedrooms); Historic interest; Luncheons, dinners, teas and snacks; Car park (30); London 137 miles, Chatsworth 10, Buxton 9, Bakewell 8.

The church of this ancient market town is known as the "Cathedral of the Peak" and visitors come from far and wide to see it. Next door, the George offers tourists to the Peak District hospitality in keeping with its history as an old coaching inn dating from 1730. All meals are served every day of the week and a wide range of appetising snacks is also obtainable over the bar. Recently used in the TV series "Yesterday's Dreams", set in this "best kept" Derbyshire village.

Devon

THE SHIP INN,
Church Street, Axmouth,
Devon EX12 4AF
Tel: 0297 21838

No accommodation; Luncheons, dinners and snacks; Car park; Seaton 1 mile.

Especially pretty on summer evenings when fairy lights twinkle in the garden trees, this fine, creeper-clad Inn extends a warm welcome at any time of year and guaranteed Devonshire hospitality. Excellent lunchtime bar food includes sandwiches, various hot dishes and daily specials, including local fish and game, and there is a more extensive evening menu. Licensee Christopher Chapman and his wife Jane are devoted supporters of Newbury Wildlife Hospital and often take in injured birds (including owls) to convalesce in the back garden (enquire about visiting hours!).

THE ANCHOR INN,
Beer, Near Seaton,
Devon EX12 3ET
Tel: 0297 20386

Accommodation (9 bedrooms, 4 with private bathroom); Free house; Dinners and snacks; Exeter 22 miles, Honiton 11, Seaton 2.

Happily free from the razzamatazz of the big Devon resorts, the little fishing village of Beer retains a sense of harmony and tranquillity that is most conducive to a relaxing and refreshing break. And these are qualities one finds in abundance at the Anchor, owned and managed by David Boalch to offer quiet, comfortable accommodation and good, wholesome food. The pretty restaurant, like many of the bedrooms, has glorious sea views and specialises in locally caught sea food; lighter meals are available in the bars, together with traditional ales. A delighful bonus is the splendid cliff-top garden where visitors may eat and drink in the long sunny Devon days. *AA**, Egon Ronay Recommended.*

GEORGE INN,
50 Old Plymouth Road, Buckfastleigh,
Devon TQ11 0DH
Tel: 0364 42708

Accommodation (7 bedrooms, all en suite); Free house; Historic interest; Luncheons, dinners and snacks; Car park (24); Totnes 5 miles.

On the southern borders of Dartmoor National Park this former coaching inn provides an excellent base for the tourist, as well as a comfortable retreat from the rigours of modern life. Beams, gleaming brasses and living fires in the bars enhance an atmosphere conducive to relaxing conversation, and well-kept ales and local ciders vie for attention with fine wines, spirits and a nice range of malt whiskies. Good local produce is skilfully transformed into mouthwatering dishes, and cream teas are served in the pretty garden. Guest accommodation is of a high standard, all en suite, with colour television, central heating and tea/coffee making facilities. A games room supplies darts, skittle alley and two pool tables.

THE OLD THATCH INN,
Cheriton Bishop, Near Exeter,
Devon EX6 6HG
Tel: 0647 24204

Accommodation (3 bedrooms, all with private bathroom); Free house; Historic interest; Luncheons, dinners and snacks; Car park (25); Exeter 10 miles.

This traditional sixteenth century inn, originally believed to have been a coaching house, is situated inside the eastern border of the Dartmoor National Park. It is ideally positioned for touring the area, with Fingle Bridge three and a half miles away, and Castle Drogo four miles. Substantial home cooked meals are served in the bar, lounge, and Traveller's Nook, with quality, choice and value for money being the key notes of the menus. The resident proprietors aim to maintain high standards whilst offering a friendly and unobtrusive service. Bed and Breakfast tariff on request. *WCTB* 🌑 🌑 🌑 *Commended, Les Routiers of the Year Award 1985/6.*

CLAY CUTTERS ARMS,
Chudleigh Knighton, Newton Abbot,
Devon TQ13 0EY
Tel: 0626 853345

Accommodation (3 bedrooms); Historic interest; Luncheons, dinners and snacks; Car park (50); Newton Abbot 4 miles.

Highly recommended in the Good Food Guide and the CAMRA Real Ale Guide, this cosy pub provides good food, draught ale and comfortable bed and breakfast. The candlelit restaurant offers a full à la carte menu, as well as traditional Sunday lunches. Interesting bar snacks are also available. Open log fires, live music and traditional pub games all contribute to the friendly atmosphere. Drinks may also be enjoyed outside in the sun garden. Private parties and wedding receptions etc are catered for – please enquire. Off the A38, take the B3344 between Chudleigh and Bovey Tracey, find us at the centre of Chudleigh Knighton village, near the church and school.

RED LION HOTEL,
The Quay, Clovelly,
Devon EX39 5SY

Tel: 02373 237

Accommodation (10 bedrooms, one with private bathroom); Historic interest; Luncheons, dinners, teas and snacks; London 214 miles, Okehampton 38, Bideford 11.

In the days when Clovelly was a thriving port this was a favourite haunt of sailors, being situated right on the beach by the old pier. The Clovelly of today is a paradise for photographers, artists and anglers, and this delightful seventeenth century hostelry blends perfectly with the quaint surroundings. All meals (and snacks) are obtainable, and excellent accommodation may be booked. Unlike many buildings in Clovelly, the Red Lion is accessible to cars (for residents only).

NEW INN,
Coleford, Crediton,
Devon EX17 5BZ

Tel: 0363 84242

Accommodation (3 bedrooms, one with private bathroom); Free house; Historic interest; Luncheons, dinners and snacks; Car park (50); Crediton 4 miles.

Inaptly named but we shall forgive it that, for this thirteenth-century former monks' retreat with its thatched roof and cob and granite walls is a veritable joy to the eye and the senses. Cosy and convivial bars serve the needs of the community and visitors alike, and an extensive blackboard menu is served lunchtime and evening in these inviting havens with their oaken beams, stone walls, open fireplaces and gleaming copper and brassware. The inn is well-known locally for the variety and quality of its food. Guest accommodation is comfortable and well appointed, and residents have the welcome facility of their own separate entrance. *Good Pub Guide, Good B&B Guide.*

THE EXMOOR SANDPIPER INN,
Countisbury, Near Lynton,
Devon EX35 6NE

Tel: 05987 263

Accommodation (11 bedrooms, all with private bathroom); Historic interest; Luncheons, dinners and snacks; Minehead 17 miles, Lynton 2.

The Exmoor Sandpiper is a fine old coaching inn, reputedly dating in part from the thirteenth and fifteenth centuries, and offering everything one would expect from a country inn — a beautiful setting amidst rolling moors, warmth and sustenance in the character bars, good food, and true hotel facilities for complete comfort. The inn's setting is truly beautiful, nestling high above Lynmouth on the coast road, with the dramatic backdrop of Exmoor. The restaurant exudes character and comfort, and offers cuisine to match, with a wide choice including seafood and lobster specialities. English or Continental breakfast can be served in the dining room or guest rooms. Accommodation too is of a high standard — all the beautifully furnished en suite rooms have colour television, radio and tea/coffee making facilities. The Exmoor Sandpiper is ideal for a quiet break or touring holiday in North Devon, with "Lorna Doone" country nearby and the beauties of the coast and Exmoor all around.

TUCKERS ARMS,
Dalwood, Near Axminster,
Devon EX13 7EG
Tel: 040488 342

Accommodation (4 bedrooms, all with shower en suite); Free house; Historic interest; Luncheons, dinners and snacks; Car park; Axminster 3 miles.

Situated beside the traditional babbling brook in the enchanted Axe Valley, this lovingly cared for hostelry has its roots in the thirteenth century, and next to the church is the oldest building in this nice little parish. Guest accommodation is today provided in four en suite bedrooms, each beautifully furnished and decorated and available at remarkably reasonable rates. Good food here attracts people from near and far, and though it is grossly unfair to single out one item from the well-planned menu, the 'Tuckers' Tiddies', pillows of puff pastry with a choice of fillings such as salmon and asparagus or steak and kidney, are absolutely *delicious!*

THE COTT INN,
Dartington, Totnes,
Devon
Tel: 0803 863777

Accommodation (6 bedrooms); Free house; Historic interest; Luncheons and dinners; Car park; Torquay 10 miles, Buckfastleigh 6, Totnes 2.

This rambling thatched inn is one of the oldest in the country (AD 1324), and is certainly one of the most beautiful. A free house, the inn is on the Buckfastleigh to Totnes turnpike road. Present-day travellers will find ample room to park their cars and relax for a while in an atmosphere of timeless charm. The cottagey bedrooms are spotless, and in addition to bed and breakfast, special terms are offered for two-day breaks (apart from all Bank Holiday periods). A superb hot and cold buffet table offers excellent refreshment at lunchtime, and during the evening there is an à la carte menu presenting home-cooked dishes using local produce. *ETB* 👑 👑 👑 *Commended.*

ROYAL CASTLE HOTEL,
The Quay, Dartmouth,
Devon TQ6 9PS

Tel: 0803 833033

Accommodation (24 bedrooms, all with private bathroom); Free house; Historic interest; Dinners and snacks; Car park (8); Plymouth 24 miles, Totnes 7.

Seven reigning monarchs have stayed at this unique quayside hotel since it began to offer hospitality and cheer in the last decade of the 16th century, and the standards which earned the Castle its Royal prefix are apparent in every aspect of its management today. Guest accommodation is sumptuous in the extreme, and all centrally heated bedrooms have private bath or shower, tea and coffee facilities, colour television, radio and direct-dial telephone. Some rooms are furnished with a magnificently draped four-poster bed, others look out over the river and bustling activity of the quay, particularly attractive as night falls and the lights of homeward bound fishing boats cast their reflections with those of the quayside buildings. Two well frequented bars offer a choice of atmosphere — the Harbour Bar, much loved by the local populace, and the Galleon with its heavy oak beams and log fires, where substantial bar fare is served. Upstairs in the restaurant, which also enjoys fine views of the river, those seeking a high quality cuisine will find a most pleasing table d'hôte menu on which locally caught fish and seafood feature prominently. Special weekend breaks provide an opportunity to sample the luxuries of this fine hotel at a reduced rate.

THE NOBODY INN,
Doddiscombsleigh, Near Exeter,
Devon

Tel: 0647 52394

Accommodation (7 bedrooms, 5 with private bathroom); Free house; Historic interest; Dinners (Tuesday to Saturday) and snacks; Car park; Exeter 7 miles, Dunsford 4.

There is always somebody in the quaintly named Nobody Inn, for it is extremely popular with visitors and locals alike, and the bars thrum constantly with friendly conversation. A typical Devonshire hostelry in typical Devonshire countryside, the inn originated in the sixteenth century as an ale and cider house for miners working nearby. Today it is a wine and whisky merchants, and it offers more sophisticated facilities but still in the warm, traditional style. A well-stocked bar with a cheerful log fire offers a variety of over 250 whiskies, including a large selection of malts, and hot and cold bar snacks are a popular order. Would-be gourmets are recommended to the à la carte restaurant where well-cooked and attractively presented food, supported by 600 fine wines, satisfy the most obdurate palate. Real old world charm is epitomised in accommodation which skilfully incorporates the most modern amenities, including showers, without spoiling the effect. The adjoining manor house, Town Barton, offers further accommodation in the Georgian style, although the house dates from the thirteenth century. All the Torbay resorts are within easy reach by car, and the edge of Dartmoor National Park is only half a mile away. Fishing and shooting with tuition if required may be arranged, whilst walkers will find this an ideal base for a variety of rambles.

ROCK INN,
Georgeham,
Devon

Tel: 0271 890322

Accommodation (3 bedrooms); Free house; Historic interest; Bar Food (7 days); Car park (40); Ilfracombe 6 miles.

As solid as its name suggests, this pleasant family-run pub stands sedately in a narrow street above Georgeham village, and offers limited but very homely accommodation in one comfortably furnished single and two double bedrooms. Even if one cannot linger overnight in this lovely corner of Devon, we must recommend a brief stop to sample the fine home-cooked fare served. There is a temptation to describe the dishes as being like mother used to make, but as that presupposes the culinary skills of one's female parent, suffice it to say they are very good indeed! Real Ales served.

GEORGE HOTEL,
Market Street, Hatherleigh,
Devon EX20 3JN

Tel: 0837 810454

Accommodation (11 bedrooms, 9 with private bathroom); Free house; Historic interest; Dinners and snacks; Car park (100); Okehampton 7 miles.

Built in 1450 as a monks' retreat, this cob and thatch pub still provides something of a quiet haven in which to refresh the spirit and calm the senses, as well as offering all the modern comforts and amenities most would be hard put to forgo today. Telephone and colour televisions are supplied in all guestrooms, some of which have en suite facilities and the luxury of four-poster bed, and decor throughout is fresh and appealing. Meals may be taken informally in the well-stocked bar, or selected from the extensive à la carte menu available in the George's rather nice restaurant. *RAC**, Egon Ronay, Good Pub Guide.*

THE FOREST INN,
Hexworthy, Dartmoor,
Devon PL20 6SD

Tel: 03643 211

Accommodation (11 bedrooms, 4 with private bathroom); Free house; Dinners and snacks; Car park (30); Ashburton 7 miles.

The Forest Inn is set amongst some of the most beautiful trekking and walking country in the South West. Easily accessible and full of Dartmoor tradition. The Forest Inn has so much to offer — Accommodation, Good Ale, Delicious Home Cooked Food, Duchy of Cornwall Fishing Permits, Horse Stabling and a very warm welcome. Children and dogs are welcomed, and facilities exist for fishing and horse riding in this area of rugged natural beauty softened by the many pretty thatched villages which nestle in protective hollows.

HOOPS INN,
Horns Cross, Bideford,
Devon EX39 5DL

Tel: 0237 451 222/247

Accommodation (14 bedrooms, 8 with private bathroom); Free house; Historic interest; Dinners and snacks; Car park (50); Bideford 5 miles.

With its thatched roof and stout white walls this enchanting old inn looks as snug as a country cat in its ideal situation midway between Clovelly and Bideford. Believed to date from the thirteenth century and once a notorious haunt of smugglers, now, under the caring eye of Derek and Marjorie Sargent, it offers both a first class base for tourists and a quiet retreat for those who would simply relax in an atmosphere of old world charm and genuine comfort. Good wholesome bar lunches and suppers are served daily and afternoon teas are readily available. An attractive restaurant provides both table d'hôte and à la carte menus in the evening. *RAC**.*

THE GROVE INN,
King's Nympton, Umberleigh,
Devon

Tel: 0769 80406

Accommodation (4 bedrooms, some en suite); Free house; Luncheons and snacks; Chulmleigh 3 miles.

An unpretentious thatched inn in pretty picturebook countryside offering good real ale and wholesome country food. The quickly-served lunchtime bar snacks are simple but nutritious, and range from soup and sandwiches (toasted or plain) to hot pasties, home made steak and kidney pie, cottage pie, pizzas, burgers, pâté and salads. The evening choice is much more extensive, and includes the Grove's "specials": home made poacher's pie, venison, duck, and steak. Tuesdays are fish-and-chips only. Traditional games include a skittle alley, shove ha'penny and dominoes.

KING'S ARMS HOTEL,
Fore Street, Kingsbridge,
Devon TQ7 1AB

Tel: 0548 852071

Accommodation (11 bedrooms, all with private bathroom); Free house; Historic interest; Luncheons, dinners and snacks; Car park (30); Plymouth 21 miles, Dartmouth 15, Totnes 13.

Hospitality, fine food, friendly service; these represent a trinity of good things at this old coaching inn, where Derek and Paula Budge must take credit for the delightful atmosphere their amenities create. Famous for its number of genuine four-poster beds, the King's Arms is a romantic hostelry in which to stay, and antiques and old photographs contribute much to its character. Nowhere is this more strikingly reflected than in the bar and restaurant area, where recent careful upgrading has been carried out. Modern amenities have also been added in the form of full central heating, tea and coffee making facilities, and an indoor swimming pool. Convivial lunchtime sessions cheer visitors and locals alike, but evening time gives the opportunity to dine elegantly by candlelight with an à la carte menu of wide choice for consideration. Restful repose is followed by a substantial English breakfast guaranteed to satisfy healthy appetites. *Member of Exechotels.* ♔♔♔

PASSAGE HOUSE INN,
Kingsteignton, Newton Abbot,
Devon

Tel: 0626 53243

No accommodation; Historic interest; Luncheons, dinners and snacks; Car park; Plymouth 31 miles, Exeter 15, Torquay 8, Teignmouth 5, Newton Abbot 2.

Discovered by "bon viveurs", this former ferry-side inn is also a favourite with racegoers visiting nearby Newton Abbot steeplechase course. Win or lose, the day will be completed in fine style by dining here, but make a reservation to avoid disappointment, such is the popularity of the restaurant, open every evening except Sunday. The menu presents a tempting and uncomplicated selection of grills, fish and poultry dishes and there are sound wines in attendance. The bar menu also offers variety in the form of seafood, poultry, casseroles, curries, grills, salads and the ubiquitous "ploughman's". Prices represent good value.

STOWFORD HOUSE HOTEL,
Lewdown, Okehampton,
Devon EX20 4BZ

Tel: 056-683 415

Accommodation (6 bedrooms, 5 with private bathroom); Historic interest; Dinners; Car park (8); Launceston 7 miles.

Stowford House Hotel, a 250-year-old former rectory, offers a warm welcome, comfortable rooms, interesting food and a tranquil garden. It is perfect for a complete rest or as a convenient holiday centre, peacefully situated within easy reach of beautiful Dartmoor and Lydford Gorge and ideal for touring North and South Devon and Cornwall. Activities available locally include riding, fishing and golf. Single, double and family rooms are available, most with en suite facilities. Children over five years of age are welcome. Guests are assured of a friendly, homely atmosphere and superb food, freshly prepared from the finest ingredients. *WCTB* ♔♔, *RAC and AA Listed, Elizabeth Gundry's "Staying Off The Beaten Track".*

RISING SUN HOTEL,
Harbourside, Lynmouth,
Devon EX35 6LQ
Tel: 0598 53223

Accommodation (16 bedrooms, all with en suite shower/bathroom); Free house; Historic interest; Luncheons, dinners and snacks; London 195 miles, Barnstaple 23, Ilfracombe 22.

An historic fourteenth century thatched smugglers' inn overlooking a small picturesque harbour and the East Lyn salmon river. The building is steeped in history, with an oak panelled dining room and bar, crooked ceilings, thick walls, and uneven oak floors. All the bedrooms have recently been refurbished to a very high standard and the roof has just been superbly re-thatched. The excellent restaurant specialises in local game and seafood. It is claimed that R.D. Blackmore wrote part of his novel 'Lorna Doone' whilst staying at The Rising Sun. The poet Percy Bysshe Shelley spent his honeymoon in 1812 in a cottage, now named after him, which is part of the hotel. It has a four-poster bed and a comfortable sitting room, and is ideal for a couple enjoying a special holiday occasion. Guests can relax in the beautifully landscaped garden which reached the finals of the U.K. Pub Garden Competition. Free fishing is available for guests on the hotel's private stretch of salmon fishing. ♛♛♛♛ *Commended, AA**, RAC** and Merit Awards. Egon Ronay, Ashley Courtenay Recommended.*

THE CROWN HOTEL,
Sinai Hill, Lynton,
Devon EX35 6AG
Tel: 059-85 2253

Accommodation (16 bedrooms, all with private bathroom; 5 four-poster); Free house; Historic interest; Dinners and snacks; Car park; London 184 miles, Barnstaple 14, Lynmouth 1.

Still retaining a delightful olde worlde atmosphere while incorporating the modern comforts expected today, this lovely eighteenth century coaching inn offers visitors a traditional high standard of food and accommodation. All rooms have private bathroom, duvets, tea and coffee making facilities, radio/alarm clocks, central heating and colour television. The restaurant offers both table d'hôte and à la carte menus, and features local seafood and fish when available. Proprietors Alan and Thelma Westgarth are closely involved with the running of The Crown and can assure guests of that personal touch so often missing today. And for a touch of luxury — what about breakfast in bed (no extra charge of course)!

Ye Olde Cottage Inne
LYNBRIDGE   LYNTON

YE OLDE COTTAGE INNE,
Lynbridge Road, Lynton,
Devon EX35 6BD
Tel: 0598 53570

Accommodation (6 bedrooms, 2 with private shower); Free house; Historic interest; Car park; Exeter 55 miles, Taunton 41, Dulverton 23, Ilfracombe 18, Minehead 18, Barnstaple 17, Lynmouth 1.

This comfortable old hostelry with its gables and leaded lights has a decidedly ecclesiastical benevolence about it. Indeed it will satisfy needs both spiritual and corporeal, for it stands high above the sea on the banks of the West Lyn River, close to some of the most beautiful walking country in England. Although of some antiquity the inn, under the personal attention of Mr J. and Mrs M. Graham, has up-to-date facilities. Moderately priced overnight accommodation is available in comfortable rooms, and central heating is installed throughout. This is a recommended spot for tours of Exmoor and the rugged North Devon coast. Opportunities for salmon and sea trout fishing exist locally.

WOODY BAY HOTEL,
Parracombe,
Devon EX31 4QX
Tel: 059-83 264

Accommodation (14 bedrooms, 13 with private bathroom); Free house; Luncheons, dinners and snacks; Car park (15); London 187 miles, Barnstaple 17, Lynton 3.

The spectacular situation of this attractive late Victorian hotel, overlooking National Trust woodland and the magnificent hogsbacked headlands of the Exmoor coastline, has attracted visitors for over a century. The appearance of the building and its surroundings has hardly changed in that time, but on the inside there are rather more bathrooms now! The table d'hote menu includes a fish dish and a vegetarian option each evening, whilst the imaginative and well-balanced a la carte menu offers further choice. The resident owners, Prue and Lawrie Scott, have created a relaxed and friendly atmosphere to complement the natural peace and tranquillity of this lovely part of Devon. This well-run hotel is also recommended by _Ashley Courtenay, Egon Ronay and Les Routiers. WCTB_ 🌸 🌸 🌸.

BABBACOMBE CLIFF HOTEL,
Beach Road, Babbacombe, Torquay,
Devon TQ1 3LY
Tel: 0222 398673 (bookings)

Accommodation (30 bedrooms, 29 with private bathroom); Free house; Historic interest; Dinners and snacks; Car park; Totnes 8 miles, Newton Abbot 6.

The Babbacombe Cliff is one of the best positioned hotels in Torbay, enjoying panoramic sea views from its two-and-a-half acres of private grounds. The hotel is noted for its associations with Oscar Wilde, who wrote some of his works here, and after whom a suite is named. Bedrooms have private bathrooms, as well as colour television and tea making facilities. Bar meals are available during normal bar opening hours, and dinners are served in the restaurant from 7.30pm. The hotel is conveniently situated only minutes from shops, theatre and beach. Special short break terms are available — for details and free full-colour brochure contact Grosvenor House, 20 St Andrews Crescent, Cardiff CF1 3DD (0222 398673).

ROYAL SEVEN STARS HOTEL,
The Plains, Totnes,
Devon TQ9 5DD
Tel: 0803 862125

Accommodation (18 bedrooms, most with private bathroom); Free house; Historic interest; Luncheons, dinners and snacks; Car park (25); London 192 miles, Exeter 25, Dartmouth 13, Torbay 6.

The Royal Seven Stars is a charming former coaching inn, dating for the most part back to 1660, and is situated in the town centre of Totnes, near the banks of the beautiful River Dart. Much refurbishment has taken place at this historic inn, including the lounge bar, and bedrooms with more private bathrooms installed. All the bedrooms now have central heating, colour television, radio, beverage tray and direct-dial telephone; some rooms have four-posters. Charges for accommodation are from £24 per person sharing a double room, and include English breakfast and VAT. The hotel is open all year and warmly welcomes guests for holidays and champagne weekend breaks. "Music Hall" evenings are held most Saturdays and these include a five-course dinner, dancing and cabaret, complete with a Music Hall chairman — all representing excellent value. *AA, RAC, Ashley Courtenay, and other leading guides.*

THE ANCHOR INN,
Lutterburn Street, Ugborough,
Ivybridge, Devon PL21 0NG

Tel: 0752 892283

Accommodation (5 bedrooms, all with private bathroom); Free house; Historic interest; Luncheons, dinners and snacks; Car park (20); Paignton 20 miles, Kingsbridge 12, Plymouth 11.

In a quiet conservation village, ideally placed just off the A38 between the South Devon coast and Dartmoor, this typical Devon "local" is a friendly place with a most atttractive lounge bar. Food is served daily in the bars from 11.30am to 1.45pm and from 7.00pm to 9.45pm, and it is advisable to book a table if possible. The wholesome fare is unpretentious and well recommended. The menu consists mainly of grills, fish and salads and there is usually a daily special on offer. Sunday midday dinners are popular, last orders being taken at 1.30pm. Visit the Anchor for a real taste of Devon.

Dorset

ILCHESTER ARMS,
9 Market Street, Abbotsbury,
Dorset DT3 4JR

Tel: 0305 871243

Accommodation (10 bedrooms, all with private bathroom); Historic interest; Luncheons, dinners and snacks; Car park (40); Weymouth 9 miles.

One charming idiosyncrasy of this old timbered hotel is that rooms are not numbered but instead are named after the flowers which grow throughout the year in its pretty, well-tended gardens, and en suite bathroom, colour television and facilities for making tea and coffee are thoughtfully provided in each. The Ilchester, centrally situated in the village and with a footpath leading from it to Chesil Beach, is particularly noted for its delicious fare which can be partaken either in the comfortable bar or in the graceful surroundings of the restaurant and conservatory where an ancient camellia tree still grows and thrives. *AA***.

ANVIL HOTEL,
Salisbury Road, Pimperne, Blandford,
Dorset DT11 8UQ
Tel: 0258 453431/480182

Accommodation (9 bedrooms, all with private bathroom); Free house (fully licensed); Historic interest; Luncheons, dinners and snacks; Car park (30); London 107 miles, Salisbury 24, Bournemouth 20.

A long, low thatched building, a garden full of lupins and roses set in a tiny village deep in the Dorset countryside – what could be more English? And that is exactly what visitors to the Anvil will find – a typical old English hostelry dating from the sixteenth century, set in an English country garden and offering good old-fashioned English hospitality. A full à la carte menu is available in the charming beamed and flagged restaurant, whilst those in a hurry will find a wide selection of bar meals in the attractive bar. Only the most hard-pressed traveller will be able to resist the temptation of morning coffee in this delightful spot! *ETB* 👑 👑 👑 👑, *RAC and AA* **.

THE RED LION,
Bourton,
Dorset SP8 5BN
Tel: 0747 840241

No accommodation; Dinners and snacks; Car park (50); Wincanton 4 miles.

We have used this well-maintained inn as a halfway house many times when journeying to and from Devon and Cornwall. With its tidy main bar bedecked with potted plants, this Badger house makes a worthwhile stop that has improved immeasurably since Mr and Mrs Gethryn Jones took over a few years ago. Two or three "specials" feature daily, meals being taken in the bar, and we recommend the home-made steak and kidney pie as delicious and of excellent value; a first-class real ale and smiling service makes a fitting accompaniment. There is a pleasant beer garden at the rear and ample car parking space.

CLOCK HOUSE HOTEL AND RESTAURANT,
Main Street, Chideock, Near Bridport,
Dorset
Tel: 0297 89423

Accommodation (6 bedrooms, some with private bathroom); Free house; Historic interest; Dinners and snacks; Car park; Bridport 3 miles.

One of the most attractive sights in this picturesque village must surely be the Clock House itself, for with its weathered walls and thatched roof it appears truly inviting. Fortunately outward appearances are not found to be deceptive, and one is just as impressed with what owners David and Lynn Aston have on offer within. Food is home cooked, plentiful and very good, whether one chooses to partake of it in the restaurant, the popular carvery, or at the bar, and a wide selection of beers, wines and spirits is available to complement it nicely. Bedrooms are comfortably furnished and equipped with beverage-making facilities, and some have private bathroom or shower. Well-mannered dogs are welcome.

THREE HORSESHOES,
Powerstock,
Dorset DT6 3TF   Tel: 030-885 328

Accommodation (4 bedrooms, 2 with private bathroom); Luncheons, dinners and snacks; Car park (40); Bridport 4 miles.

This is a difficult pub to pass by — and indeed perhaps the only creatures who do so with ease are the cows which amble up the village street at milking time! Attractive in the extreme with large gardens to the rear, the Shoes as it is affectionately known has a solid and well-earned reputation for good home cooking, and local fish dishes are a speciality on the menu here, together with Dorset lamb, beef and game in season. Those in search of a comfortable bed and traditional English breakfast will find four comfortable, well cared for guest rooms at their disposal.

LANGTON ARMS,
Tarrant Monkton, Blandford,   Tel: 025-889 225
Dorset DT11 8RX   Fax: 025-889 480

Accommodation (6 bedrooms, all with private bathroom); Free house; Historic interest; Dinners and snacks; Car park (60); Blandford 4 miles.

So many people wanted to stay the night here after enjoying the facilities of bars, beer garden and skittle alley that it seemed the sensible thing to go ahead and build accommodation — and the modern, beautifully fitted guest bedrooms provide a sharp and in no way displeasing contrast to the old-world charm of this seventeenth-century thatched pub. All six double rooms have television, private bathroom, telephone and calming rural view, and individually controlled heating ensures one's comfort at all times. Food is served in the bars at lunchtime and throughout the evening, and blackboard specials supplement the usual menu which includes home-cooked chilli, shepherd's pie, steak and kidney pudding and good grills. A wide range of cask and keg beers are available, usually with guest ales, and they go down particularly well on Wednesdays — "Curry Night" at the Langton Arms. On Thursday the speciality cooking is Chinese, Monday is "French Night" and Tuesdays and Fridays have an Italian flavour with traditional pizzas offering a choice of fillings. A popular restaurant opening nightly and for Sunday lunch caters for more formal dining, and when the occasion is extra special a telephone call generally ensures that any reasonable extra special requirement is met. *Egon Ronay, Good Pub Guide.*

Durham

TEESDALE HOTEL,
Market Square, Middleton-in-Teesdale,
Co. Durham DL12 0QG

Tel: 0833 40264

Accommodation (14 bedrooms, 11 with private bathroom); Free house; Historic interest; Luncheons, dinners and snacks; Car park; Barnard Castle 8 miles.

Traditions of hospitality here go back to the days when coaches, not cars, rolled under the stone archway to the safety of the yard beyond. Conveniently situated at the heart of this riverside Pennine village, the Teesdale Hotel has an atmosphere of friendliness and good cheer which proves as great an attraction as the first class cooking and comfortable, well furnished accommodation. Colour television and radio are provided in all guest rooms, most of which have private bathroom, and for those seeking greater freedom and who have at least three nights to spare, luxury cottages are available in the courtyard. Both restaurant and bar food is served. *AA, RAC, Egon Ronay, Which, Northumbria Tourist Board.*

THREE HORSE SHOES INN,
Running Waters, Sherburn House,
Co. Durham DH1 2SR
Tel: 091 3720286

Accommodation (6 bedrooms, 3 with private bathroom); Free house; Luncheons, dinners and snacks; Car park (50); Durham 4 miles.

Charming hosts Gary and Christine Davis describe the Three Horse Shoes as a comfortable old country inn with a well-stocked cellar, good food and first-class accommodation — and really, that just about sums it up! Guest rooms are attractive indeed, prettily furnished and all with colour television, tea-making facilities, central heating, and private shower and washbasin. Continental breakfast is available if preferred, but the full English breakfast must be recommended, for it is a truly memorable experience. Evening meals, lunches and bar snacks are served, and the menu includes such delights as individual home-made steak and kidney pies and succulent steaks.

DUN COW INN,
43 Front Street, Sedgefield,
Co. Durham TS21 3AT
Tel: 0740 20894/5

Accommodation (6 bedrooms); Free house; Historic interest; Luncheons, dinners and snacks; Car park (25); Durham 10 miles, Stockton-on-Tees 8.

If I were a producer in search of picturesque locations I should take note of the Dun Cow, for its flower-decked, fresh painted exterior would certainly look delightful on film. Inside it is no less pleasing to the eye, with pretty matching fabrics in guestrooms (all with colour television and telephone), and a comfortably old fashioned air. There is a wide choice of bar food, and an extensive à la carte menu is offered in the restaurant. Breakfast deserves a special mention for quantity as well as quality, and is timed to suit guests, not just staff.

A lily pond in a glade of Epping Forest, Essex.

Essex

THE QUEEN'S HEAD,
Fordstreet, Aldham,
Near Colchester, Essex

Tel: 0206 241291

No accommodation; Free house; Historic interest; Luncheons, dinners and snacks; Car park (100); Ipswich 18 miles.

On the A604 between the old Roman town of Colchester and Halstead, this friendly free house provided us with good company and wholesome sustenance. It has a large car park and a beer garden popular with family parties. The Queen's Head's cuisine, as we were to find out, is noted for its imaginative home-cooked food, the menu highlighting a different speciality daily. The selection of wines is surprisingly large. Snacks are obtainable in the bar and real ales on offer include several local tipples. There is much of historic interest in this peaceful area, including a number of imposing churches and country houses, as well as Constable's incomparable Dedham Vale. The inn possesses good facilities for private functions.

YE OLDE WHITE HARTE HOTEL,
The Quay, Burnham-on-Crouch,
Essex CM0 8AS

Tel: 0621 782106

Accommodation (15 bedrooms, 11 with private bathroom); Free house; Historic interest; Luncheons, dinners and snacks; Car park (15); London 45 miles, Southend 24, Chelmsford 20.

The fact that this charming old freehouse is so popular with the boating fraternity is good recommendation of its fare — for appetites worked up on the estuary are not easily satisfied! Freshly prepared and attractively presented food is available both in the restaurant and in the eating area of the bar, and the company is invariably cheerful and convivial. Those wishing to linger a while in these parts will find sensibly priced, well-kept guest rooms, some with private facilities and all furnished to a most acceptable standard of comfort. The inn enjoys a central situation overlooking the busy yachting centre of Burnham. 👑 👑 👑, *.

Gloucestershire

Please mention
Recommended WAYSIDE INNS
when seeking refreshment or
accommodation at a Hotel
mentioned in these pages

VILLAGE PUB,
Barnsley, Cirencester,
Gloucestershire GL7 5EF

Tel: 028 574 421

Accommodation (6 bedrooms, 4 with private bathroom); Free house; Luncheons, dinners and snacks; Car park (40); Cirencester 4 miles.

Very much what the name suggests and proudly so, this popular inn offers comfortably furnished and nicely decorated guestrooms (some with en suite facilities) to those in search of a bed for the night, and a hearty English breakfast will be found on rising. Food is served in both bar and restaurant and daily specials supplement a menu which includes fresh-caught local Bibury trout, grilled with butter, home-made chilli-con-carne, and a substantial ten-ounce sirloin steak, charcoal-grilled to perfection. A sheltered courtyard provides for al fresco dining and well-kept real ales are served.

KINGSHEAD HOUSE RESTAURANT,
Birdlip,
Gloucestershire GL4 8JH

Tel: 0452 862299

Accommodation (one bedroom with private bathroom); Free house; Historic interest; Luncheons (Tues.-Fri. and Sundays), dinners (Tues.-Sat.), snacks (Tues.-Fri.); Car park (12); Gloucester 6 miles, Cheltenham 5.

Accommodation here is limited to just one spacious, comfortable en suite bedroom, making those fortunate enough to have secured it feel more like visiting friends of Warren and Judy Knock than actual paying guests. Open nightly except Sunday and Monday, the locally popular restaurant boasts a carefully chosen menu offering old favourites as well as new and interesting dishes. Luncheon may also be taken in the restaurant Tuesday to Friday and on Sunday, or if one prefers, less formal fare is served in the bar. Situated on the Cirencester to Gloucester road, this former coaching inn dates back to the 1700s. *ETB* 👑👑, *BTA Commended 1990.*

THE CROWN HOTEL,
High Street, Blockley, Moreton-in-Marsh,
Gloucestershire GL56 9EX

Tel: 0386 700245

Accommodation (21 bedrooms, including 4 four-poster rooms and 2 suites, all with private facilities); Free house; Historic interest; Luncheons, dinners and snacks; Car park (50); Moreton-in-Marsh 3 miles.

These lovely old Cotswold villages seem to radiate warmth from the very stones of their honey-coloured cottages, and this fine Elizabethan inn on Blockley's High Street is no exception. Generous helpings of good food, real ale and a blazing fire welcome winter visitors, whilst those enjoying a summer tour or day trip can eat outdoors in the old coachyard or take a seat at the front and watch the world go by. Children welcome. *ETB* 👑 👑 👑 👑, *AA***, RAC, Egon Ronay, Michelin.*

THE OLD NEW INN,
Bourton-on-the-Water,
Gloucestershire GL54 2AF

Tel: 0451 20467

Accommodation (24 bedrooms, 8 with private bathroom); Historic interest; Luncheons, dinners and snacks; Car park (30), Garages (6); London 85 miles, Gloucester 24, Stow-on-the-Wold 4.

The only trouble with a stay at this gracious establishment is that one is tempted to prolong it indefinitely! Set on the banks of the River Windrush and with charming secluded gardens, the hotel has been run by the Morris family for over fifty years and much has been done to create the friendly, relaxed atmosphere that makes one feel thoroughly at home. Bedrooms are cosy and comfortable, some being available with private facilities, and there is a television room and two lounges exclusively for residents, although many visitors may find themselves drawn to the four public bars where darts or conversation may be enjoyed. A bright and attractive dining room is the setting for a good table d'hôte dinner menu, and light lunches and bar snacks are served at midday.

THE COLESBOURNE INN,
Colesbourne, Near Cheltenham,
Gloucestershire GL53 9NP

Tel: 024-287 376
Fax: 024-287 397

Accommodation (10 bedrooms, all with private bathroom); Historic interest; Luncheons, dinners and snacks; Car park (70); Gloucester 8 miles.

This 200-year-old inn, situated in the Cotswold countryside, retains all its traditional charm, while offering guests a high standard of comfort and service. All bedrooms have en suite facilities, colour TV, telephone and tea-making facilities. Home grown produce is used in the recently extended restaurant, whilst the bar has local ale and real log fires. Golf is available in the area, and the countryside is particularly suitable for walking. Ideally situated for exploring the Cotswolds by car. Patio and rear lawn; large car park. You will get a warm welcome and super food! *ETB* 👑 👑 👑 *Commended, AA Specially Selected Inn, RAC 2 Tankards, Egon Ronay, Les Routiers, Good Beer Guide.*

WILD DUCK INN,
Ewen, Near Cirencester,
Gloucestershire

Tel: 0285 770310/770364

Accommodation (9 double bedrooms, all with private bathroom); Historic interest; Free house; Luncheons and dinners; Car park (50); Chippenham 18 miles, Cheltenham 16, Swindon 16, Tetbury 9, Cirencester 3, Kemble Station 1.

Nestling in delightful, unspoilt Gloucestershire countryside, this is an old inn of outstanding character, with original beams and inglenook open fires giving a traditional atmosphere of warmth and friendliness. Food is of the highest quality, with an extensive menu operating at lunchtime and in the evenings. Bar lunches are also available. Two bedrooms have four-posters and overlook the delightful, award-winning garden. All nine rooms have private bath and shower en suite, colour television, tea/coffee making facilities and telephone, making this a desirable overnight or weekly holiday base, in addition to being an enchanting place to quench one's thirst. 👑 👑 👑, *RAC****.

FOX INN,
Great Barrington,
Gloucestershire OX8 4TB

Tel: 045-14 385

Accommodation (5 bedrooms); Historic interest; Luncheons and snacks; Car park (30); Cheltenham 20 miles, Stow-on-the-Wold 12, Burford 4.

Serenely placed in a quiet village in the lovely Windrush Valley, this homely little hostelry is well worth visiting during the course of a Cotswold tour. The inn is easily reached, being only a short distance off the A40 just a few miles west of Burford. Hosts Pat and Bill Mayer extend a friendly welcome and provide a good range of hot and cold snacks in the bar at lunchtime and in the evening. There are four double guest rooms and one single, providing good overnight accommodation at most reasonable rates, with reductions for stays of four nights or more.

NOTE

All the information in this book is given in good faith in the belief that it is correct. However, the publishers cannot guarantee the facts given in these pages, neither are they responsible for changes in policy, ownership or terms that may take place after the date of going to press. Readers should always satisfy themselves that the facilities they require are available and that the terms, if quoted, still apply.

BLACK HORSE INN,
North Nibley, Near Dursley,
Gloucestershire

Tel: 0453 546841

Accommodation (6 bedrooms, 5 with private shower room); Luncheons, dinners and snacks; Car park (20); Dursley 2 miles.

This tastefully modernised old coaching inn is situated in superb walking country beneath the Tyndale Monument and on the Cotswold Way. Appetising bar meals will tempt the hungry walker whilst à la carte restaurant meals will satisfy larger appetites. Six comfortable bedrooms, equipped with television, telephones and hot drinks facilities, beckon the tired traveller and there are traditional games such as darts in the friendly bar, as well as a garden for children to play in. *ETB* 🏆 🏆*, RAC listed.*

THE GEORGE,
St. Briavels, Lydney,
Gloucestershire GL15 6TA

Tel: 0594 530228

Accommodation (2 bedrooms); Free house; Historic interest; Snacks; Car park (20); Gloucester 19 miles, Chepstow 9.

An eleventh-century Celtic coffin lid discovered on removal of a fireplace is displayed next to the bar counter of this traditional and welcoming hostelry overlooking the castle moat, but any gloomy thoughts it might engender are immediately dispelled by the excellent menu, which features such favourites as homemade steak and kidney pie, lasagne, sausage and garlic bread and fresh local trout. Limited overnight accommodation is available and visitors fortunate enough to have secured a room will find comfortable beds, pleasant furnishings and tea and coffee facilities thoughtfully provided. A large centrally-heated bathroom with bath and shower is just a few steps down the corridor.

OLD STOCKS HOTEL,
The Square, Stow-on-the-Wold,
Gloucestershire GL54 1AF

Tel: 0451 30666 Fax: 0451 870014

Accommodation (17 bedrooms, all with private bathroom); Free house; Historic interest; Dinners and snacks; Car park (14); London 84 miles, Stratford-upon-Avon 21, Cheltenham 18.

The charming old town of Stow-on-the-Wold lies in the heart of the Cotswolds, and those seeking overnight accommodation here could do no better than the Old Stocks Hotel, whose tasteful guest rooms are in keeping with the establishment's old world character. Cotswold stone walls and oaken beams contrast with modern amenities of telephone, tea/coffee facilities, colour television, radio, hairdryer and en suite bathroom. Three superior rooms are also available, providing an even greater range of comforts. Excellent table d'hôte and à la carte menus are offered in the spacious and elegant dining room, featuring such joys as the excellent Old Stocks pork casserole, tender chicken chasseur and mouth-watering steak and kidney, as well as a tempting range of vegetarian dishes. Special bargain breaks are available and the resident proprietors, Alan and Caroline Rose, will be happy to give advice on exploring this enchanting area.

OLD FARMHOUSE HOTEL,
Lower Swell, Stow-on-the-Wold,
Gloucestershire GL54 1LF

Tel: 0451 30232

Accommodation (15 bedrooms, 13 with private bathroom); Free house; Historic interest; Dinners and snacks; Car park (30); Stow-on-the-Wold 1 mile.

A sixteenth century Cotswold stone farmhouse in a peaceful hamlet one mile west of Stow-on-the-Wold, now sympathetically converted to a warm and comfortable small hotel of 15 bedrooms, all individually decorated, including two four-posters. It is well situated for touring, exploring and sound sleeping, and has the relaxed and informal air of its farmhouse origins. The resident owners place much emphasis on the quality of the food, and real hospitality. Breakfasts are full cooked English, while evening menus include both table d'hôte and à la carte, with a choice of traditional and varied dishes. Vegetarians are welcome. Colour TV, radio/alarm, telephone and tea/coffee facilities are in all bedrooms. Centrally heated, with log fires. Secluded wall garden, and ample private parking. There is a range of short term breaks, weekday and weekend, throughout the year. *ETB* 👑 👑 👑, *AA 2 Stars, Good Hotel Guide, Egon Ronay.*

HORSE AND GROOM INN,
Upper Oddington, Moreton-in-Marsh,
Gloucestershire   Tel: 0451 30584

Accommodation (7 bedrooms, all with private bathroom); Free house; Historic interest;
Luncheons, dinners and snacks; Car park; Stow-on-the-Wold 2 miles.

In the very heart of the Cotswolds, this sixteenth century inn, with its genuine old-world bars
and inglenook fireplace, offers the ideal break. Its situation provides the perfect opportunity to
explore the villages, historic buildings and places of interest in this delightful area. Guests of all
ages are welcomed by Russell, Steve, Alison and Tina. All bedrooms are en suite, centrally
heated, and have hot drinks facilities and colour television. Excellent traditional English food
is served in the bar and cosy dining room. This is a fine place for families, with a beer garden
and a children's paddock. Winter break terms available. *ETB* 👑👑, *AA Listed.*

SWAN HOTEL,
14 Market Street, Wotton-under-Edge,
Gloucestershire GL12 7AE   Tel: 0453 842329

Accommodation (16 bedrooms, all with private bathroom); Free house; Luncheons, dinners and
snacks; Stroud 9 miles.

Decorated outside with gay-coloured hanging baskets and inside with shining brass and
copperware, this old hostelry with its exposed stone walls, open fires and timbered ceilings is
as attractive as it is comfortable. All guest accommodation is en suite and the charmingly
furnished, centrally heated bedrooms are provided with colour television and telephone.
Dinner may be taken either in the picturesque Cotswold Restaurant (where a dinner dance is
held every Saturday evening) or in the less formal and moderately priced Grill Room, which
also serves as a pleasant lunch venue. A good range of refreshment is on offer both in lounge
and in continental wine bar. *RAC**.*

> PLEASE ENCLOSE A STAMPED
> ADDRESSED ENVELOPE WHEN
> WRITING TO ENQUIRE ABOUT
> ACCOMMODATION FEATURED IN
> THIS GUIDE

Hampshire

THE MILBURYS,
Beauworth, Near Cheriton,
Hampshire SO24 0PB

Tel: 0962 79248

Accommodation (4 bedrooms, 3 with private bathroom); Free house; Historic interest; Luncheons, dinners and snacks; Car park (70); London 61 miles, Basingstoke 17, Winchester 8.

The restaurant at Milburys has won praise from many a gourmet, but if you have omitted to book and find yourself regretfully turned away, don't despair. An extensive menu is also presented daily in the bar, where perhaps escargot in butter, followed by grilled sirloin garni and rounded off with hazelnut meringues will make up for your disappointment. A 300-foot well is situated in the bar with a safety grid covering it. Ice cubes can be dropped and a spotlight will show that it takes nearly 9 seconds to reach the bottom. A massive treadwell draws water up, and it is said that King Stephen's treasure was hidden there!!! Well worth a visit! There are four comfortable bedrooms, including a family suite, and Friday to Sunday weekend breaks are especially good value.

THE COMPASSES INN,
Damerham, Fordingbridge,
Hampshire SP6 3HQ

Tel: 072-53 231

Accommodation (4 bedrooms); Free house; Historic interest; Luncheons, dinners and snacks; Car park; Fordingbridge 3 miles.

A perfect example of the traditional English country inn, the Compasses is an unpretentious rural hostelry offering excellent value for money and a really warm welcome. Comfortable accommodation, with a choice of single, double or family rooms, all with washbasins, is available. Good, wholesome and substantial meals are offered, either in the dining room or at the bar, where guests may enjoy a selection of real ales, including Wadworth 6X, with the accompaniment of a traditional jazz band on Fridays. Picnic lunches, too, are an additional service offered at the Compasses, and will be greatly appreciated by those intending to tour the New Forest, the River Avon or the ancient town of Cranborne nearby, with its famous Chase, scene of many a royal hunt.

NEW FOREST INN,
Emery Down, Lyndhurst,
Hampshire SO43 7DY

Tel: 0703 282329
Fax: 0425 480704

Accommodation (4 bedrooms, all with private bathroom); Luncheons and dinners (Sundays), snacks; Car park; Lyndhurst 1 mile.

Do take note of the unusual front lounge porchway, which is formed of the caravan that for many years stood on this site selling beer in the days when no licence was necessary. Today this delightful hostelry boasts a menu which provides for all tastes and pockets, and ranges from wonderfully satisfying home-made soups and sandwiches to such temptations as venison sautéed gently in red wine, tender veal cooked in sherry and cream, and steaks which yield instantly to the knife. Comfortable, well-appointed guest rooms await those seeking accommodation and a hearty breakfast is included in the charge. *Les Routiers, "Which" Pub Guide.*

CART AND HORSES,
Kings Worthy, Near Winchester,
Hampshire

Tel: 0962 882360

No accommodation; Historic interest; Dinners and snacks; Car park; Winchester 2 miles.

A short way off the M3 (Junction 9), just north of Winchester where the A33 and A34 meet, this handsome inn fully deserves its obvious popularity. Look out for the old cart on display outside. This charming place is a recommended port of call for families who are free to use a paved terrace at the rear of the converted barn, now a functions room-cum-skittle alley. The lawns, with plenty of tables, are popular in summer where parents can relax whilst their offspring cavort in a safely enclosed play area with Wendy house, slide, swings, adventure course and trampolines. With luck, parents may escape temporarily to the comparative tranquillity of the old beamed bar. Food of the uncomplicated variety is available at mid-day and in the evening.

HIGH CORNER INN,
Linwood, Near Ringwood,
Hampshire BH24 3QY

Tel: 0425 473973

Accommodation (7 bedrooms, all with private bathroom; self-contained woodland chalet); Free house; Historic interest; Dinners and snacks, also Sunday carvery; Car park; Southampton 18 miles, Bournemouth 17.

A lovely, typically English, early 18th century inn in the very heart of the New Forest, the High Corner Inn gave us a warm feeling of pleasurable anticipation by its very appearance. We were not disappointed; whilst enjoying a leisurely aperitif, we were confronted with a difficult decision in making a lunchtime choice from a wide-ranging bar snacks menu. After a starter, we chose the grilled Avon trout with almonds and a homemade fruit pie to follow. The meal was delicious and we were tempted to return later for an à la carte dinner served in a charming little restaurant. There are rooms for families with children, and a woodland garden. 🏆🏆🏆 Commended. Egon Ronay, Les Routiers Recommended.

THE ROYAL OAK,
North Gorley, Near Fordingbridge,
Hampshire SP6 2PB

Tel: 0425 652244

No accommodation; Historic interest; Snacks; Car park (50); Fordingbridge 2 miles.

In the heart of the New Forest and surrounded by common land, this neat and tidy thatched hostelry dates from the 17th century and is a wonderful place to take the family for refreshment with good food, drink and entertainment of the wildlife variety to captivate all ages. At one time a hunting lodge, this hospitable retreat overlooks a large duck pond whilst nearby is a field with donkeys. Behind the inn is a sizeable and well-kept garden with tables and sun umbrellas and diversions for the children in the form of swings and a climbing frame.

GEORGE HOTEL,
High Street, Odiham,
Hampshire RG25 1LP

Tel: 0256 702081
Fax: 0256 704213

Accommodation (18 bedrooms, all with private bathroom); Historic interest; Luncheons (Sunday), dinners (not Sunday or Monday), snacks; Car park (30); Basingstoke 7 miles.

The George has presided over Odiham's broad High Street since the fifteenth century, and a wall painting dating from 1500 can still be seen in one of the bedrooms. Accommodation is in comfortable, attractively furnished guest rooms, all with private bathroom, tea and coffee facilities, telephone and colour television, and two exceedingly elegant four-poster rooms are also available. Dinner is served Tuesday to Saturday inclusive in the George's popular restaurant, and each lunchtime and evening the bar offers a good and varied menu which includes lasagne, chilli, beef and mushroom pie and steaks as well as toasted sandwiches, jacket potatoes and tempting sweets. *ETB ❦ ❦ ❦ ❦ Commended, AA**.*

SHIP INN,
Owslebury, Near Winchester,
Hampshire SO21 1LT

Tel: 096-274 358
(changing early 1991 to 0962 777358)

No accommodation; Historic interest; Snacks (not Sunday); Car park; Winchester 4 miles.

Tile-hung and with tubs of flowers decorating its facade, this 17th century hostelry has an attraction that is hard to ignore. We had no intentions of doing so in any event and on entering discovered a most interesting bar complete with inglenook fireplace, old pillars and beams and with several intimate alcoves ideal for quiet conversation or romantic 'tête-à-têtes'. Bar food was of the fairly basic variety but nonetheless good and reasonably priced, meals being served every day except Sundays. There is a small room where those with children may sit but on clement days, relaxation and refreshment in the delightful back garden is recommended. The views of the surrounding countryside are magnificent and there are swings and a climbing frame to amuse the youngsters.

WHITE HART INN,
High Street, Stockbridge,
Hampshire SO20 6HF

Tel: 0264 810475

Fax: 0264 810268

Accommodation (14 bedrooms, 9 with private bathroom); Free house; Historic interest; Dinners and snacks; Car park; London 68 miles, Salisbury 15, Winchester 9.

Old and new are well met at this deceiving establishment, which from the front appears to be just a cosy country pub. Stop off, however, and the truth becomes apparent, for behind the homely facade are facilities and comforts which would not be found wanting by the most discerning of visitors. Well furnished and attractively decorated bedrooms are available both in the converted stable block which provides motel-style accommodation and in the refurbished original building, all having television, central heating and tea and coffee facilities, and those in the stable block with private bathroom. A fine and well deserved reputation is enjoyed by Shavers Restaurant, where daily specials supplement the good à la carte menu and service and presentation are as pleasing as the fare, freshly prepared to individual tastes. Those who cannot devote the time such cuisine demands will find a wide selection of meals and snacks readily available in the bar, where some real ales are still drawn from the wood and delight the connoisseur. Stockbridge itself stands on the River Test, widely considered the best trout stream in England, and the White Hart can arrange fishing as well as golf, shooting, walking and tours of the area.

BOURNE VALLEY INN,
St Mary Bourne, Near Andover,
Hampshire SP11 6BT

Tel: 026473 8361

Accommodation (11 bedrooms, all with private bathroom); Free house; Historic interest; Luncheons, dinners and snacks; Car park (40); Whitchurch 3 miles.

Children are particularly welcomed at this mid nineteenth-century redbrick hostelry, and a well-equipped play area is provided for them in the spacious riverside gardens. Bar food is available at all times and a good vegetarian menu is offered in the restaurant in addition to the à la carte which features a nicely balanced mix of French and English cuisine. Guest accommodation comprises single, twin and double bedrooms, with one family suite, and all rooms are en suite and have television, radio, tea-maker, hairdryer, safe and trouser press. Residents have the added amenity of a quiet and comfortable private lounge in which to relax.
♕ ♕ ♕

WELLINGTON ARMS HOTEL,
Stratfield Turgis, Near Basingstoke,
Hampshire RG27 0AS

Tel: 0256 882214
Fax: 0256 882934

Accommodation (15 bedrooms, all with private bathroom); Free house; Historic interest; Luncheons, dinners and snacks; Car park (50); Basingstoke 6 miles.

The first thing to strike one on crossing the threshold of this lovely old establishment is the air of calm and tranquillity, as if one has left behind the hurly-burly of the world and entered a place of charm and serenity. Guest rooms are individually furnished, each having en suite facilities, colour television, telephone and tea and coffee tray, and the thoughtful touches of sweet jar, writing paper and hairdryer alert one immediately to the kind of caring service which can be expected during a stay. Cuisine is on a par with accommodation, and good bar food is available in addition to the delights on offer in the restaurant. *Egon Ronay, Michelin.*

Herefordshire

WHITE HART INN,
Aston Crews, Near Ross-on-Wye,
Herefordshire
Tel: 098-981 203

No accommodation; Free house; Historic interest; Luncheons, dinners and snacks; Car park; Newent 4 miles.

Focal point of a small, rural village community, this attractive old inn is delightfully placed between the Royal Forest of Dean and the mountains of Wales. The beams and huge open fireplace in the main bar hint at a history extending back 400 years and these features are instrumental in giving this friendly place an atmosphere as relaxed as its surroundings. There is a comfortable new 46-seater dining room where a varied range of dishes is on offer at lunchtime and in the evening, including several vegetarian dishes. Our verdict is that for city dwellers seeking the ideal place in which to wind down, this is the perfect answer. *Egon Ronay Recommended.*

RED LION HOTEL,
Bredwardine,
Herefordshire HR3 6BU
Tel: 09817 303

Accommodation (10 bedrooms, all with private bathroom); Free house; Historic interest; Dinners and snacks; Car park (35); Hereford 11 miles.

This easily spotted red brick building stands in its own well-kept grounds in the centre of Bredwardine, with the Black Mountains towering to the west, and eastwards the gentle Malvern Hills. The old world charm of public rooms, enhanced by antiques, oaken beams and open fireplaces, is complemented well by the excellent modern amenities of guest bedrooms, all individually furnished to a high degree of comfort and equipped with tea and coffee facilities and colour television. Guests may partake of the evening meal in the pleasant dining room which is wonderfully served in fresh produce by the local estate, or alternatively may choose from a varied bar menu.

THE GREEN MAN,
Fownhope,
Tel: 0432 860243
Herefordshire HR1 4PE
Fax: 0432 860207

Accommodation (15 double bedrooms, all with private bathroom, 1 four-poster, 3 family, 1 single; self-catering cottages); Free house; Historic interest; Luncheons, dinners and snacks; Car park (75); Gloucester 24 miles, Monmouth 22, Ross-on-Wye 9, Hereford 7.

This ancient black and white timbered inn provides an ideal base for exploring the beautiful surrounding countryside and nearby places of interest. There are two bars, an oak-beamed restaurant, a buttery for bar snacks and a large attractive garden. The resident proprietors place great emphasis upon the quality of food and an informal and friendly atmosphere. An extensive bar food menu is available mornings and evenings, and dinners à la carte are served in the restaurant. Bedrooms all have colour television, radio alarm, direct-dial telephone, tea/coffee making equipment, central heating and many extras. Two well-equipped self-catering cottages, accommodating four and six adults, are also available, with colour television, microwave, auto-washing machine etc. *ETB* 👑👑👑👑, *AA**, RAC**, Les Routiers, Egon Ronay.*

FEATHERS HOTEL,
High Street, Ledbury,
Tel: 0531 2600/5266
Herefordshire
Fax: 0531 2001

Accommodation (11 bedrooms, all with private bathroom); Free house; Historic interest; Dinners and snacks; Car park; Worcester 16 miles, Gloucester 16, Hereford 14.

One need not search long for this charming old hostelry, for the black and white one-time coaching inn built in the days of Elizabeth I is very much a landmark on the market town's main street. An interesting selection of bar food is on offer here with traditional ales and cider to wash it down, and more formal tastes are well catered for in the restaurant with good à la carte and table d'hôte menus and a nice wine list. Visitors are comfortably accommodated in individually decorated bedrooms, all with private bathroom, remote control television, tea-making facilities and telephone. *ETB* 👑👑👑👑, *AA***.*

THE ROYAL OAK HOTEL AND THE MERMAID SEAFOOD RESTAURANT,
The Southend, Ledbury,
Herefordshire HR8 2EY

Tel: 0531 2110
Fax: 0531 4761

Accommodation (11 bedrooms, 8 with private bathroom); Free house; Historic interest; Dinners and snacks; Car park (20); Forest of Dean 18 miles, Worcester 16, Hereford 14, Malvern 8.

This old Coaching Inn dates in part to the early 1400s. The main building was built around 1530 and is timber framed; in 1820 the Georgian facade was added. Today the inn retains all its character but offers the visitor every modern convenience. Homemade bar and restaurant meals are available, plus fine ales. All the rooms are double glazed, with central heating, colour television and complimentary beverage tray. Ledbury is an ideal location from which to visit the cathedral cities of Hereford, Gloucester and Worcester and the Forest of Dean, all within 25 minutes' drive. The town of Ledbury has many historic buildings and associations with famous literary figures such as Elizabeth Barrett Browning and John Masefield, once Poet Laureate. Close by is the famous Eastnor Castle and Deer Park, and there are magnificent views and walks in the Malvern Hills. 👑 👑 👑.

YE OLDE FERRIE INNE,
Symonds Yat West,
Herefordshire HR9 6BL

Tel: 0600 890 232

Accommodation (9 bedrooms, 6 with private bathroom); Free house; Historic interest; Luncheons, dinners and snacks; Car park (60); Gloucester 24 miles, Ross-on-Wye 8, Monmouth 4.

This attractive 15th century inn stands on the banks of the River Wye. All bedrooms and the renowned Steak Restaurant overlook the river with superb views of the Wye Valley. Free fishing and ferry crossing available to residents. Balloon trips, golf and pony trekking can also be arranged, or just enjoy the beautiful riverside and forest walks. Dinner in the oak-beamed restaurant in front of a roaring log fire is one of the special pleasures of an out-of-season break, or a good bar snack menu caters for smaller appetites. Special mid-week and Autumn Break tariff available. 👑 👑 👑 *Approved.*

Hertfordshire

TWO BREWERS,
The Common, Chipperfield, Kings Langley, Hertfordshire WD4 9BS

Tel: 0923 265266
Fax: 0923 261884

Accommodation (20 bedrooms, all with private bathroom); Free house; Historic interest; Luncheons, dinners and snacks; Car park (40); London 22 miles, Watford 6.

Once a training establishment for the boxing fraternity of the day, the Two Brewers faces the Common of this picturesque English village and dates from the late 1600s. Well appointed guest bedrooms all have private bathroom, colour television, radio, telephone and tea and coffee facilities, and decor is fresh and appealing. Both table d'hôte and à la carte menus are offered in the restaurant where service is discreet and efficient, and vegetarians are as well catered for as those who prefer the delights of tender roast lamb, succulent steaks, game, poultry and beautifully prepared fish dishes. Leisure weekends at special rates are a good introduction to the attractions of the area. *RAC***, AA**.*

Humberside

THE FLEECE INN,
Bishop Wilton, Near York, Humberside YO4 1RU

Tel: 075-96 251

Accommodation (6 bedrooms); Free house; Dinners and snacks; Car park (20); York 10 miles.

Set in the picturesque and unspoilt village of Bishop Wilton on the edge of the Yorkshire Wolds, the Fleece Inn is a fine touring base with much to see locally, including the city of York and the east coast. And after a long day's walk on the moors, what could be more relaxing than to return to a satisfying, freshly-prepared meal and a glass of good, traditional, hand-pulled beer? The Fleece has a wide range of good beers and fine wines to be enjoyed on their own or with your bar meal — served at lunchtime and in the evenings — or your dinner in the dining room. Overnight accommodation is available in six cheerful and spotlessly clean bedrooms, to be followed by a hearty breakfast to set you up for the next day.

Isle of Wight

CLARENDON HOTEL AND WIGHT MOUSE INN,
Chale,
Isle of Wight PO38 2HA

Tel: 0983 730431

Accommodation (14 bedrooms, 8 with private bathroom or shower); Free house; Hot meals and drinks all day; Car park (200); Newport 9 miles, Ventnor 7.

Our Hotel, The Clarendon, is a 17th century Coaching Inn of immense charm and character enjoying an enviable reputation for excellent food, wine, comfort and hospitality. Standing in its own lovely grounds, it overlooks the magnificent West Wight coastline. Children are very welcome, at reduced rates, and we are a few minutes from Blackgang Chine and several beautiful beaches. We have absolutely everything for your comfort. All rooms have colour televisions and all bathrooms hairdryers. **Our Pub, The Wight Mouse Inn,** which is attached to the hotel has recently been awarded the Egon Ronay Family Pub of the Year Award. It has great atmosphere, open fires, real ales, 365 different whiskies, excellent meals and live entertainment nightly all year round and is open all day every day for meals and drinks. Golf, Shooting, Fishing, Horse Riding and Hire Cars can all be easily arranged. *Egon Ronay Family Pub of the Year 1990, AA, RAC**, Les Routiers, CAMRA and Ashley Courtenay Recommended.*

Kent

HOUSE OF AGNES HOTEL,
71 St Dunstans Street, Canterbury,
Kent CT2 8BN
Tel: 0227 472185 Fax: 0227 464527

Accommodation (All rooms with private bathroom); Free house; Historic interest; Luncheons, dinners and snacks; London 58 miles, Dover 15.

The House of Agnes Hotel, which is named afer a Charles Dickens heroine (Agnes Wickfield from the novel *David Copperfield*), is a lovely Tudor building set against the historic backdrop of the City of Canterbury. Modern facilities ensure the comfort of guests without spoiling its old world ambience. The hotel has full central heating, and all rooms are en suite, with colour television, tea/coffee making facilities and direct-dial telephone. The intimate restaurant offers both à la carte and table d'hôte menus and is open to non-residents. For a relaxing drink there is a small, comfortable bar with traditional English beer, high quality lager and a full range of wines and spirits. A marquee is available for large lunch parties up to 65 persons, and hotel and coach bookings can also be arranged. There is a private car park and a garden.

Please mention
Recommended WAYSIDE INNS
when seeking refreshment or
accommodation at a Hotel
mentioned in these pages

CARPENTERS ARMS,
The Street, Eastling,
Kent ME13 0AZ

Tel: 079-589 234

Accommodation (4 bedrooms, all en suite); Historic interest; Luncheons, dinners and snacks; Faversham 4 miles.

A cosy and relaxing village pub which dates from the fourteenth century, the Carpenters Arms is run by Tony and Mary O'Regan, who have improved and upgraded its already ample facilities. The popular restaurant offers a good menu from noon till 2.30 p.m. and again from 6.30 until 10.30 p.m., Monday to Saturday, with a traditional roast being served Sunday lunchtime. All dishes are freshly prepared to order, so could not be termed "fast food", but the beautifully cooked steaks, poultry and seafood are worth waiting for. The vegetarian too is well served, with a delicious choice of dishes to tempt even meat-eaters.

The Harrow Inn, Warren Street, Nr Lenham, Maidstone, Kent.

THE HARROW,
Warren Sreet, Near Lenham,
Kent ME17 2ED

Tel: 0622 858727

Accommodation (7 bedrooms, 4 with private bathroom); Free house; Historic interest; Dinners and snacks; Car park (30); Maidstone 10 miles, Charing 5, Lenham 2.

The Harrow is situated high on the North Downs of Kent amidst lush farmland. Once the forge and rest house for travellers en route to Canterbury, it has now been converted to a comfortable country inn. It offers visitors good food and a comfortable night's stay in one of the well-appointed bedrooms, all with fine views of the downland countryside. All the tastefully furnished rooms have colour television, telephone, clock radio and tea/coffee making facilities. The Harrow is centrally heated throughout with additional log fires in winter. Eating here is very popular with both residents and locals — either in the lounge bar or in the quieter, secluded restaurant overlooking the garden. To accompany your choice from the special, regular or à la carte menus there is a fine selection of wines. The Harrow is conveniently situated for visiting historic Canterbury, the Cinque Ports and many other places of interest in the area. *RAC Acclaimed, AA Listed, Egon Ronay Recommended.*

THE BULL HOTEL,
Wrotham, Near Sevenoaks,
Kent TN15 7RF

Tel: 0732 885522

Accommodation (9 bedrooms, 6 with private bathroom); Free house; Historic interest; Car park (70); London 27 miles, Maidstone 11, Sevenoaks 7.

The Bull Hotel has been standing since the fourteenth century in the ancient village of Wrotham, and was once a stopping-off point for pilgrims on their way to Canterbury. Today it offers spacious and comfortable accommodation and superb cooking to travellers, businessmen and holidaymakers. All rooms are centrally heated, and have colour television and tea-making facilities. The restaurant, open to non-residents, serves a wide selection of meals and snacks, complemented by a carefully chosen wine list. The inn is ideal as a base for those wishing to visit the many places of interest in the area, as it is only just off the M20 and the M25/26. It is also an excellent stop-over point midway between the Channel ports, Gatwick and London. 👑 👑 👑

Lancashire

BARBON INN,
Barbon, Via Carnforth,
Lancashire LA6 2LJ

Tel: 046 836 233

Accommodation (9 bedrooms); Free house; Historic interest; Dinners and snacks; Car park (10); Kirkby Lonsdale 3 miles.

Just twenty minutes from the M6, this seventeenth-century inn could be in quite another world where concrete and cares and rushing vehicles seem like something from a science fiction film. Accommodation is comfortable and well appointed, most rooms being equipped with colour television, tea and coffee facilities and electric blankets, and bathrooms are so well placed that the lack of private facilities proves no hardship. Bar meals are available in the evening as well as at lunchtime for those who would deny themselves the pleasure of a five-course dinner served in the well recommended dining room.

HODDER BRIDGE HOTEL,
Chaigley, Near Clitheroe,
Lancashire BB7 3LP

Tel: 025-486 216/717

Accommodation (5 bedrooms, 2 with private bathroom); Free house; Historic interest; Luncheons, dinners and snacks; Car park (60); Blackburn 12 miles.

Those with a weight problem are definitely NOT recommended to this old world, family owned freehouse unless, that is, they are strongwilled enough to resist the temptations of the hotel's Oliver Twist Carvery where, unlike the Dickensian character, they will be cordially urged to have some more. Those who give in to the succulent sugar-baked hams, the ribs of beef, roast pork and tender turkeys could perhaps do penance by walking off the extra pounds in this charming countryside of the Hodder River and Valley. Comfortable accommodation is available and good food is served nightly in the bar.

HARK TO BOUNTY INN,
Slaidburn, Clitheroe,
Lancashire BB7 3EP

Tel: 020-06 246

Accommodation (8 bedrooms, 7 with private bathroom); Historic interest; Luncheons and dinners; Car park (10); Skipton 25 miles, Clitheroe 7.

This solid old inn was once the seat of the Bowland Forest Court, and anyone giving it a trial today will be well pleased with both accommodation and cuisine. All en suite guest bedrooms are furnished comfortably and have tea-making facilities and colour television. Local maps and guides may be consulted in the relaxing residents' lounge. The oak-beamed bar is a popular haunt with locals as well as tourists, and serves excellent bar meals together with real ale, with a more substantial cuisine to be found in the highly commended restaurant. The area has much of interest for the visitor and good fishing is available locally.

Leicestershire

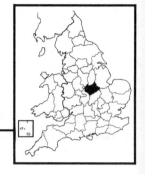

MARQUESS OF EXETER HOTEL,
Lyddington, Near Uppingham,
Leicestershire LE15 9LR

Tel: 0572 822477
Fax: 0572 821343

Accommodation (17 bedrooms, all with private bathroom); Free house; Historic interest; Luncheons, dinners and snacks; Car park (80); Leicester 27 miles, Kettering 13.

Close to Rutland Water, this fine sixteenth-century coaching inn is a careful blend of old world character, quality cuisine and smart, beautifully appointed accommodation which caters well for tourist and businessman alike. The usual range of bar meals and snacks is served between 12.15 and 1.45pm and again from 7.15 until 10pm in the snug beamed bar, and the traditionally furnished restaurant is open Monday to Friday lunchtime and Monday to Saturday evening, offering a choice of à la carte and table d'hôte menus, as well as for Sunday luncheon. En suite bathroom, trouser press, hairdryer, direct-dial telephone, beverage facilities and colour television are standard in all the tastefully decorated bedrooms. Two suites with private lounge are available.

RAM JAM INN,
Great North Road, Stretton,
Leicestershire LE15 7QX

Tel: 0780 410776
Fax: 0572 724721

Accommodation (8 bedrooms, all with private bathroom); Free house; Historic interest; Luncheons, dinners and snacks; Car park; Stamford 8 miles.

Smart motel-style accommodation is provided at this beautifully refurbished, long established inn, with all rooms having remote control colour television, radio alarm and tea and coffee facilities in addition to well-appointed private bathrooms. The snack bar is open from 7.00 am until 7.00 pm to provide quick and tasty sustenance to those in a hurry, delicious hot and cold meals are offered at the bar, and a quality restaurant ensures that more formal requirements are met. In all areas the emphasis is on fresh, good quality ingredients, simply cooked. Children are made welcome and the major credit cards are accepted.

Lincolnshire

NEW ENGLAND HOTEL,
Wide Bargate, Boston,
Lincolnshire PE21 6SH

Tel: 0205 365255 Fax: 0205 310597

Accommodation (25 bedrooms, all with private bathroom); Luncheons, dinners and snacks; Lincoln 35 miles, King's Lynn 34, Skegness 22.

Popular with business travellers, tourists and locals alike, this warmly welcoming hotel stands at the heart of Boston, a good base from which to explore the ancient town and the flat, but by no means featureless, countryside beyond. Colour television, telephone and beverage-making facilities are provided in the 25 en suite guestrooms, and the Carving Table Restaurant offers a fine cuisine which includes continental dishes, as well as good roast rib of English beef and succulent steaks served plain or with interesting sauces. It was from Boston that the Pilgrim Fathers set sail, and the town is still a busy and thriving port.

CROWN HOTEL,
West End, Holbeach,
Lincolnshire PE12 7LW

Tel: 0406 23941

Accommodation (8 bedrooms, 5 with private bathroom); Free house; Historic interest; Luncheons, dinners and snacks; Car park (20); King's Lynn 19 miles.

With several real ales on offer in the horse-shoe shaped bar, including Bass and Adnams, our visit was a convivial one. We were introduced to the pleasures of the cosy (and almost full) restaurant where diners were considering the varied fare with enthusiasm. Top price on the à la carte menu was only in the region of £10, and our duckling with all the trimmings represented excellent value. Also remarkably light on the pocket is wholesome overnight accommodation and full English breakfast. En suite facilities are available and all rooms have colour television, central heating, washbasins and tea-makers. The Crown is obviously going places, judging from extension plans for a new functions room and 12 motel units.

BROWNLOW ARMS,
Hough-on-the-Hill,
Lincolnshire NG32 2AZ

Tel: 0400 50234

Accommodation (5 bedrooms, all with private bathroom); Free house; Historic interest; Sunday lunches, dinners (not Sunday) and snacks; Car park (45); Grantham 7 miles.

It is difficult to decide whether this 17th-century inn is at its most pleasing in winter or in summer — the answer doubtless depending on whether one prefers the idea of a delicious homecooked meal and a drink on the secluded patio or in front of a well stacked log fire in the snug bar. Comfortable accommodation is available throughout the year should one be tempted to linger a while in this charming spot, and colour television and tea and coffee facilities are provided in all of the nicely furnished guestrooms. Those who prefer restaurant dining will find an extensive à la carte menu presented in an intimate and romantic atmosphere. 👑👑👑

GEORGE HOTEL,
Leadenham,
Lincolnshire LN5 0PN

Tel: 0400 72251

Accommodation (7 bedrooms, 2 with private bathroom); Free house; Historic interest; Luncheons (Sunday), dinners and snacks; Car park (200); Lincoln 13 miles.

No less than five hundred varieties of whisky are to be found in the aptly named Scotch Lounge of this homely country pub, situated midway between Newark and Sleaford on the A17 and just eight miles from the A1. Accommodation for overnight guests is in the quiet cottage behind the hostelry, and the reasonable rate for comfortably furnished room with television and tea-maker includes a substantial full English breakfast on rising. Good bar food is served at lunchtime and evening each day, and the Tudor Restaurant specialises in a traditional English cuisine which has earned it a reputation far beyond the immediate area. *Les Routiers, Good Pub Guide.*

London

YE OLDE WINDMILL INN,
South Side, Clapham Common,
London SW4 9DE

Tel: 081-673 4578

Accommodation (13 bedrooms, one with private bathroom); Historic interest; Dinners and snacks; Car park (20); City centre 3 miles.

Real inns are sadly a rarity in the capital nowadays, but this large, Victorian-fronted building standing at the edge of Clapham Common now thankfully goes some way towards filling the gap. The bars are spacious and are decorated in true Victorian style, with dark wood and stained glass: fine surroundings in which to enjoy a glass of good beer, perhaps with something from the lunchtime buffet bar. The Windmill's restaurant serves food at lunchtimes and on weekday evenings, and the full range of traditional inn facilities is completed with the availability of modern, comfortable bedrooms and a choice of tasty breakfasts. A pleasant outdoor arbour takes full advantage of the inn's position by the Common.

> PLEASE ENCLOSE A STAMPED
> ADDRESSED ENVELOPE WHEN
> WRITING TO ENQUIRE ABOUT
> ACCOMMODATION FEATURED IN
> THIS GUIDE

Norfolk

THE HOSTE HOTEL,
The Green, Burnham Market,
Norfolk

Tel: 0328 738257

Accommodation (8 bedrooms, all with private bathroom); Historic interest; Luncheons, dinners and snacks; Cromer 26 miles, Fakenham 10.

In the peaceful heart of Lord Nelson's Norfolk, this seventeenth century hotel, the oldest in the district, stands on the green of a beautiful, unspoilt Georgian village. The name "Hoste" derives from Captain Sir William Hoste, a protégé of Lord Nelson and at one time lord of the manor. Under the management of Wendy Watkins, an award-winning master chef, the hotel now boasts eight elegant bedrooms, two with four-posters, and each individually designed to enhance the original seventeenth century features. They are fully en suite, and have colour television and private phone. The restaurant has become one of the most popular and fashionable in the area, using the best of fresh ingredients, naturally cooked. Nearby is Burnham Overy Staithe, ideal for sailing and birdwatching, and Holkham Hall, home of the Cokes of Norfolk. There are three bird sanctuaries, sailing clubs, golf courses and tennis courts in the area. Sailing lessons and fishing trips can be arranged.

THE KING'S HEAD HOTEL,
Dereham,
Norfolk NR19 1AD

Tel: 0362 693842
Fax: 0362 693776

Accommodation (15 bedrooms, 12 with private bathroom or shower); Historic interest; Luncheons, dinners and snacks; Car park (30); London 105 miles, Newmarket 43, Cromer 27.

In these days of standardisation and uniformity it is most refreshing to find in The King's Head a fine example of a good old-fashioned English hotel alive and well in that most English of counties — Norfolk. Essentially a family concern, the seventeenth-century hotel, now thoroughly modernised, is run by the Black family to maintain the highest standards of comfort, courtesy and good, wholesome English cooking carefully prepared and complemented by an extensive wine list. All the bedrooms are centrally heated with tea/coffee facilities, radio room-call, colour television, telephone, and some have en suite facilities. *AA/RAC **.*

BARTON ANGLER
COUNTRY INN

BARTON ANGLER COUNTRY INN,
Irstead Road, Neatishead, Wroxham,
Norfolk NR12 8XP   Tel: 0692 630740

Accommodation (7 bedrooms, 5 with private bathroom); Free house; Historic interest; Dinners
(Thurs./Fri./Sat. only), snacks; Car park (60); Wroxham 4 miles.

If 'country inn' has connotations of a simple village pub offering clean but unpretentious accommodation, don't be deceived. The Barton Angler has all the friendly informality of such a place, but decor, furnishings and facilities throughout are of a standard which will satisfy the most demanding of tastes. Richly draped four-poster beds grace two of the seven guest bedrooms, all of which except the singles are en suite, and colour television, tea and coffee facilities, direct-dial telephone and baby listening service are thoughtfully provided. Throughout the winter months a welcoming log fire supplements the central heating in the bar, and it is in this convivial place that one learns more about the area than any guidebook will have to impart. A most pleasing selection of bar fare is on offer here, in the evening as well as at lunchtime to cater for those whose appetites are unequal to the cuisine served in the elegant and locally renowned restaurant. Owned by the Nature Trust, Barton is one of the least spoilt of the Broads, and the inn can hire out boats to allow one to explore it at leisure. It was here, incidentally (in its former rectory days) that Lord Nelson stayed whilst learning to sail.

THE BOAR INN,
Great Ryburgh, Fakenham,
Norfolk NR21 0DX

Tel: 032-878 212

Accommodation (4 bedrooms); Free house; Dinners and snacks; Car park (20); Fakenham 3 miles.

Standing opposite the round towered Saxon church in the quiet little village of Great Ryburgh is the Boar Inn where visitors can discover the pleasures of relaxation and rest, qualities fast disappearing in today's increasingly frenzied world. The Boar is a free house, and a fine glass of real ale can be enjoyed with your choice of a range of bar snacks. Restaurant meals are also served in the evening. Those who wish to linger in this lovely area can take advantage of the Boar's comfortable accommodation, and there are many places of interest in the surrounding area, including Sandringham, Holkham Hall and Pensthorpe Wildfowl Centre.

THE FERRY INN,
Reedham, Norwich,
Norfolk NR13 3HA

Tel: 0493 700429

No accommodation; Free house; Luncheons, dinners and snacks; Car park; Norwich 17 miles, Acle 6.

Broads holidaymakers are drawn to this friendly old inn alongside the River Yare primarily for its impressive array of liquid and dry refreshments. The main bar is invariably abuzz with convivial chatter and, all around, are interesting artifacts from all walks of life. Parents may relax and rest assured — there is a sun lounge where children are most welcome. The Inn has good moorings and a launching ramp for craft up to 35ft in length. By boat, or by car, we may confirm that visitors are made to feel very much at home here. Indeed, some take advantage of the fact by patronising the on-site caravan and camping park.

THE HARE ARMS,
Stow Bardolph,
Norfolk PE34 3HT

Tel: 0366 382229

No accommodation; Historic interest; Dinners (not Sundays) and snacks; Car park; Downham Market 2 miles.

Essentially a traditional country inn, an integral part of a quiet Norfolk village complete with church, smithy, 'big house' and farms, the Hare Arms deserves elevation in its description because it is a very special place boasting the accolade of being the most popular pub and restaurant for miles around, the latter presenting a surprisingly sophisticated international cuisine. The reasons are simple to fathom — excellent food, beer and wine, relaxed atmosphere (no canned music), cheerful and efficient service and the warm welcome extended by Mine Hosts, David and Tricia McManus. A wide variety of bar food is served at lunchtime and in the evening and, in summer, the lawn is a favourite place for families. The inn also has first-rate facilities for functions. *Egon Ronay "Star" entry for Pub Food.*

SCOLE INN,
Scole, Near Diss,
Norfolk IP21 4DR

Tel: 0379 740481

Accommodation (23 bedrooms, all with private bathroom); Free house; Historic interest; Luncheons, dinners and snacks; Car park (60); Diss 2 miles.

Built by a wealthy Norfolk wool merchant in the mid 17th century, this Grade I listed building has a history as elaborate as its wonderfully carved oak staircase! Charles II and Lord Nelson are among the notable personages claimed as guests — and more notorious than notable, highwayman John Belcher used the inn as his headquarters over 200 years ago. Though today's clientele is perhaps less colourful, the character and atmosphere of the Scole Inn has changed little over the centuries, and it is a joy indeed to the traditionalist, with its wealth of heavy oak doors and beams and inglenook fireplaces in which logs crackle cheerfully on days when the weather is unkind. Food served in the elegant dining room is of the highest quality and includes some East Anglian speciality dishes well worth sampling. Visitors without the time to do such cuisine justice will find wholesome, freshly prepared bar meals and snacks available throughout opening hours. Overnight guests can be accommodated in the main building or in the recently converted stable block, and all well appointed rooms have colour television, trouser press, hairdryer and central heating. En suite facilities are provided in most rooms.

SUTTON STAITHE INN,
Sutton Staithe, Near Stalham, Norwich,
The Broads, Norfolk

Tel: 0692 80244

Accommodation (10 bedrooms, 6 with private bathroom); Free house; Historic interest; Luncheons, dinners and snacks; Car park; Norwich 17 miles, Great Yarmouth 15.

Such was the disreputable reputation of this quiet little inn hidden away in a corner of the Broads that it lost its licence in the last century, no doubt because its clientele seems to have been made up principally from poachers and smugglers! Happily, however, this was restored in the 1930s and now, under the care of the Taylor family, the Sutton Staithe enjoys a growing reputation for good food and a friendly welcome in peaceful surroundings. The bar food includes light snacks such as sandwiches, rolls and ploughman's lunches with hot dishes including lasagne and cottage pie. A full à la carte menu is featured in the Decoy Restaurant. *ETB* 🏆 🏆 🏆.

LIFEBOAT INN,
Ship Lane, Thornham,
Norfolk PE36 6LT

Tel: 048-526 236

Accommodation (13 bedrooms, all with private bathroom); Free house; Historic interest; Dinners and snacks; Car park (120); Hunstanton 4 miles.

A lovely, 16th century traditional English inn, a little out of the way but well worth finding, the 'Lifeboat', once the haunt of smugglers, is today some little way from the sea but the briny is still within sight in the distance. The bar with its low ceiling, pillars and uneven floor, conjured up visions of the unhurried life of years gone by as we sampled an excellent pint of real ale and tucked into our fisherman's pie. A number of other rooms lead off the bar where families may sit. There is also a spacious conservatory adjoining a patio with tables and a children's slide. Food is wholesomely home-made and a small restaurant is open evenings only. *Egon Ronay, Good Pub Guide; Beer, Bed and Breakfast, Good Beer.*

THE OLD RAM PUBLIC HOUSE,
Ipswich Road (A140), Tivetshall St Mary,
Norfolk NR15 2DE

Tel: 037-976 8228

No accommodation; Free house; Luncheons, dinners and snacks; Car park (80); Harleston 6 miles.

This attractive 17th-century roadside dining pub has been refurbished by John Trafford to give several elevated eating areas, lit by over-table Tiffany lamps in bold pinks and greens, with fresh Sanderson print draperies, comfortable upholstered seating, including a newly designated non-smoking dining room. The spacious main room has red brick floors, stripped beams and standing-timber dividers, a huge log fire in the brick hearth, a longcase clock, and ceilings hung with antique craftsmen's tools. An intimate dining room known as the Coach House boasts intimate pew seating, leading to a gallery featuring Victorian copper and brassware. The emphasis is very much on food, with some tables reserved on weekdays. There are seats on the flower-enclosed terrace and lawn garden behind. No dogs. *Egon Ronay Recommended.*

CROWN HOTEL,
Wells-next-the-Sea,
Norfolk NR23 1EX

Tel: 0328 710209

Accommodation (15 bedrooms, 9 with private bathroom); Free house; Historic interest; Luncheons, dinners and snacks; Car park; Norwich 31 miles, Fakenham 10.

Snug in its secluded tree-dotted square, the Crown enjoys a peaceful setting while being only minutes from the harbour of this quaint little Norfolk town. Guest rooms are beautifully appointed with colour television and beverage-making facilities, and cuisine is as pleasing as accommodation, with meals offered in the attractive sun lounge as well as in bar and popular restaurant, where fresh, locally caught seafood is a speciality on the nightly changing menu. Proprietor Wilfred Foyers lived for a time in France, and says his aim in the Crown was to combine the best of the family-run *auberge* with good English pub hospitality. He has succeeded admirably! 👑 👑 👑, **.

Northumberland

BLUE BELL HOTEL,
Belford,
Northumberland NE70 7NE

Tel: 0668 213543

Accommodation (17 bedrooms, all with private bathroom); Free house; Historic interest, Dinners and snacks; Car park; Alnwick 15 miles.

Less than a mile from the A1, this creeper-clad, early eighteenth-century hotel enjoys a central position near to the old Market Cross in Belford village. Guest rooms are furnished in elegant Georgian style, and all have shower or bath en suite, colour television, beverage-making facilities, telephone and hairdryer. The finest local lamb, seafood and game is complemented by fresh produce straight from the inn's extensive vegetable garden, and meals may be partaken of in the restaurant or less formally in the comfortable bar. Children are catered for with a special menu, and are accommodated free when sharing with two adults.

COTTAGE INN,
Dunstan Village, Craster,
Northumberland NE66 3SZ

Tel: 0665 76658

Accommodation (17 bedrooms, 10 with private bathroom); Free house; Luncheons (Sunday), dinners and snacks; Car park (30); Alnwick 10 miles.

Snug in five acres of garden and woodland, this especially nice and recently modernised inn functions under the watchful eye of proprietors Larry and Shirley Jobling, who do all that can reasonably be expected of good hosts to ensure that a stay here is memorable indeed. Particularly suitable for the disabled, accommodation is all on one level, and reasonably priced standard rooms, comfortably furnished and with tea and coffee trays, are available in addition to the en suite guestrooms with the added facility of television. The atmospheric Harry Hotspur Restaurant, decorated with murals by a local artist, is a pleasing setting in which to dine after a day's adventuring in this wonderfully unspoilt corner.

KNOWESGATE HOTEL,
Kirkwhelpington,
Northumberland NE19 2SH

Tel: 0830 40261

Accommodation (16 bedrooms, all with private bathroom); Free house; Dinners and snacks; Car park; Otterburn 9 miles.

This small, stone-built, family-run hotel stands on the edge of the National Park. It is ideally situated for walking and touring Northumberland, the Scottish Borders and local National Trust properties. All bedrooms have private bathrooms, colour television and tea-makers. Some ground floor rooms are available. *AA **.*

ANGLERS ARMS,
Weldon Bridge, Longframlington,
Northumberland

Tel: 0665 570655

Accommodation (5 bedrooms, all with private bathroom); Historic interest; Luncheons, dinners and snacks; Car park; Rothbury 5 miles.

Fishing on the nearby River Coquet is free to residents of this traditional Northumbrian inn, built in the 1700s and situated in an area so beautiful it will lift the most dejected spirit. Tastefully decorated bedrooms, all with private facilities and one with four-poster bed, await the overnight guest, and a hearty North Country breakfast sets one up for a day on the river or discovering the delights of this unspoilt county. Bar meals are served during opening hours and those who wish a truly memorable culinary experience are recommended to the à la carte restaurant and Pullman railway carriage, where the only problem encountered is making a choice from the extensive menu.

OLDE SHIP HOTEL,
Seahouses,
Northumberland

Tel: 0665 720200

Accommodation (12 bedrooms, all with private bathroom); Free house; Luncheons, dinners and snacks; Car park (12); Berwick-upon-Tweed 22 miles, Alnwick 14.

Old-fashioned in a sense, this homely old inn was originally built as a farmhouse in the mid-eighteenth century. The Olde Ship stands above the picturesque harbour and has a long established reputation for excellent food and drink. Because of the nautical theme throughout one may be tempted to linger longer in this fascinating hostelry. All guest rooms are en suite and have telephone and satellite colour television. Mr and Mrs A.C. Glen personally supervise the well-being of their guests, and for a holiday break in convivial surroundings this little place has much to commend it. Courtesy coach from local station.

THE HADRIAN HOTEL,
Wall, Near Hexham,
Northumberland NE46 4EE

Tel: 0434 681232/681236

Accommodation (9 bedrooms, 4 with private bathroom); Free house; Historic interest; Luncheons, dinners and snacks; Car park (60); Newcastle-upon-Tyne 20 miles.

The village of Wall has the distinction of being built almost entirely of stones taken from the nearby Hadrian's Wall, and this creeper-clad little hotel stands at the southern end of the village, only a few minutes from the Roman Wall itself, and offering fine unrestricted views over the local countryside. Good beer and a comprehensive selection of bar snacks ensure that the refreshment needs of visitors are catered for, while the hotel's dining room with its fine food, and the comfortable bedrooms, mean that those wishing to stay overnight — or longer — can fully enjoy this real "find" in one of the last unspoilt areas of the country.

BATTLESTEADS HOTEL,
Wark-on-Tyne, Hexham,
Northumberland NE48 3LS

Tel: 0434 230209

Accommodation (7 bedrooms, all with private bathroom); Free house; Dinners and snacks; Car park (50); Newcastle-upon-Tyne 27 miles, Hexham 12.

Well-placed for those wishing to visit unspoilt Northumberland is this comfortable little hotel, run by resident proprietors Robert and Doris Rowland and offering service which is both friendly and efficient. This is a perfect place to enjoy a glass of good beer and a tasty snack, with a pleasant garden and views of the surrounding countryside. Bedrooms (all with colour television) are well appointed and spick and span, and the hotel offers an excellent base for those wishing to visit Hadrian's Wall, the Kielder reservoir and forest, historic houses and castles, and the nearby beauty spots and places of interest.

Please mention
Recommended WAYSIDE INNS
when seeking refreshment or
accommodation at a Hotel
mentioned in these pages

Oxfordshire

THE KING'S HEAD INN AND RESTAURANT,
Bledington, Near Kingham,
Oxfordshire OX7 6HD
Tel: 0608 658365

Accommodation (9 bedrooms, all with private bathroom); Free house; Historic interest; Luncheons, dinners and snacks; Car park (60); Stow-on-the-Wold 4 miles.

Facing Bledington's village green with its brook and ducks (all known locally by name!) stands the King's Head Inn, an establishment which has echoed with the sounds of convivial hospitality for over four centuries. Bledington nestles in the heart of the Cotswolds and is in easy reach of Stratford, Bourton-on-the-Water and Burford. The charming accommodation is in keeping with the atmosphere, all bedrooms having en suite bathroom, TV, telephone and hot drinks facilities. High quality and inventive bar fare is served at lunchtimes, with full à la carte in the restaurant in the evenings. Real ale is served in the two bars with their inglenook fireplaces, original beams, and a garden room and garden add to this delightful old inn. *ETB* ♛ ♛ ♛.

LAMB INN,
Sheep Street, Burford,
Oxfordshire OX8 4LR
Tel: 099382 3155

Accommodation (16 bedrooms, 13 with private bathroom); Free house; Historic interest; Dinners and snacks; Car park (8); Gloucester 29 miles, Oxford 20, Stow-on-the-Wold 10.

We heard the Lamb described by some overseas visitors as "a typical old English inn" — but perhaps it would be fairer to say it is typical of what one imagines an old English inn to be, with its heavy oaken beams, brass and copperware, flagged floor, log fires and antiques that seem almost to whisper the secrets of their past. Country-cottage guestrooms are wonderfully comfortable and well appointed, and cuisine offers the best of British produce skilfully prepared and served with loving attention to detail. Light lunches are available in bar or garden, weather permitting, and dinner is a leisurely experience in the candlelit, pillared dining room. *ETB* ♛ ♛ ♛ ♛.

BELL HOTEL,
Church Street, Charlbury,
Oxfordshire OX7 3AP

Tel: 0608 810278
Fax: 0608 811447

Accommodation (14 bedrooms, all with private bathroom); Free house; Historic interest; Luncheons, dinners and snacks; Car park (30); London 71 miles, Oxford 15.

Much improved and upgraded since its former coaching days, the Bell enjoys a central situation in this charming old "hill town of free men" as the name translates. Guest rooms are full of character and provide the welcome facilities of colour television, tea tray, hairdryer and telephone, as well as having private bathrooms. A wide range of food is available — from snacks in the bar with its log fire and flagstone floor, to the oak-beamed restaurant's full à la carte menu which caters admirably for growing vegetarian tastes in addition to offering the best of beef, lamb, poultry, fish and game. *ETB* 👑 👑 👑 👑, *AA and RAC **, Michelin, Egon Ronay.*

COACH AND HORSES,
Chislehampton,
Oxfordshire OX9 7UX

Tel: 0865 890255

Accommodation (9 bedrooms, all with private facilities); Free house; Historic interest; Luncheons and dinners; Car park (40); Oxford 7 miles.

Tranquilly situated in the village of Chislehampton, the Coach and Horses does well for those who wish to be within easy reach of Oxford and its many pleasures while enjoying rural quiet at night. Nine chalet-style bedrooms were recently added to this sixteenth-century hostelry, and as well as being individually heated and provided with colour television, radio, telephone and en suite facilities, decor throughout is charmingly pretty with well chosen colours and matching fabrics. Both table d'hôte and à la carte menus are presented in the restaurant, and in summer months tables on patio and lawn make a pleasant spot for a drink. Snacks are available at weekend lunchtimes.

SHEPHERDS HALL INN,
Witney Road, Freeland,
Oxfordshire OX7 2HQ

Tel: 0993 881256

Accommodation (5 bedrooms, all with private bath or shower and toilet); Free house; Historic interest; Luncheons, dinners and snacks; Car park; Oxford 12 miles, Witney 4, Woodstock 4.

One of the finest houses for miles, the welcoming Shepherds Hall stands in an area famed for its sheep rearing, hence its name. Rooms are now modernised, with colour TV and tea/coffee making facilities, yet retain the atmosphere of a true country inn, and proprietors Liz and David Fyson present a comprehensive selection of appetising meals and snacks in the bar every day. This is a good place to bring the family (perhaps after visiting Woodstock and Blenheim Palace) for there is an attractive beer garden and children's play area. Wholesome accommodation is available at reasonable rates and this includes a full English breakfast.

OLD GEORGE INN,
The Greens, Leafield,
Oxfordshire OX8 5NP

Tel: 099-387 288

Accommodation (2 bedrooms, both with private bathroom); Free house; Historic interest; Luncheons, dinners (not Tuesday), snacks; Burford 5 miles.

This charming village inn is situated on the green in the lovely Cotswold village of Leafield. On the edge of Wychwood Forest, which was once used by Henry VIII for hunting. There is a sports centre at Witney, five miles away; other places of interest nearby include Blenheim Palace, Burford, and a Wild Life Park. The comfortably furnished bedrooms have televisions. Delicious meals are served in the restaurant, and bar snacks are also available. *Les Routiers.*

THE OLD SWAN,
Minster Lovell,
Oxfordshire OX8 5RN
Tel: 0993 774441

Accommodation (18 bedrooms, all with private bathroom); Free house; Historic interest; Luncheons, dinners and snacks; Car park (60); Oxford 15 miles, Witney 3.

The Old Swan, which dates from around 1390, lies tucked away in the picturesque Cotswold village of Minster Lovell, beside the River Windrush. With its polished flagstone floors and open log fires, it retains its historic charm while offering all the luxury comforts expected by today's guests. All the individually furnished bedrooms have private bathrooms, telephone and colour television, with a magnificent four-poster room for that special occasion. The comfortably furnished public rooms are ideal for relaxing or enjoying a quiet drink. With the emphasis on fresh produce and imaginative menus, fine cuisine can be sampled in the impressive setting of the beamed, candlelit restaurant. The Swan is surrounded by beautiful countryside and is ideal for exploring the Cotswolds and visiting Oxford, Cheltenham and many other places of interest. *AA ***, Egon Ronay.*

THE BELL,
Shenington, Banbury,
Oxfordshire OX15 6NQ
Tel: 0295 87 274

Accommodation (4 bedrooms, one with private bathroom); Free house; Luncheons, dinners and snacks; Banbury 6 miles.

A solid and welcoming hostelry set on the edge of the Cotswolds, this early eighteenth-century inn is worth a visit even if Shenington isn't exactly on one's itinerary, for a short diversion is a small price to pay for the delicious fare on offer here every day and each evening except Sunday. All dishes are home-made and freshly prepared to order and specialities on the daily changing menu include hearty casseroles, seafood, pasta and game in season. Should one wish to sample breakfast as well as lunch or dinner, overnight accommodation is available in four charming guest rooms, and one is pleased to note that no supplement is in force for the single.

KINGS ARMS,
Skirmett, Near Henley-on-Thames,
Oxfordshire
Tel: 049-163 247

Accommodation (4 bedrooms, 2 with private bathroom); Free house; Historic interest; Luncheons, dinners and snacks; Car park; Henley-on-Thames 6 miles.

Deep in the countryside in a tranquil, slightly isolated setting, the Kings Arms is the perfect antidote to busy roads and crowded city pubs! Here comfortable chairs, inglenook fireplace, high beamed ceilings hung with jugs and tankards and, of course, plenty of good real ale, create a sense of old world warmth and conviviality. Bar meals are available seven days a week and an à la carte menu is available in the pretty candlelit restaurant on four evenings.

SHAVEN CROWN HOTEL,
Shipton-under-Wychwood,
Oxfordshire OX7 6BA

Tel: 0993 830330

Accommodation (9 bedrooms, all with private bathroom); Free house; Historic interest; Luncheons (Sundays), dinners and snacks; Car park (20); Burford 4 miles.

Designed around a courtyard garden in which one may lunch al fresco in the summer months, the six-hundred-year-old Shaven Crown was originally hospice to Bruern Abbey and is built of that local honey-coloured stone which mellows so beautifully with the centuries. En suite guest bedrooms are provided with colour television and tea and coffee facilities, and as much care has been taken with their decor and furnishings as with those of the comfortable public rooms. Imaginative bar food is served every lunchtime and evening and an excellent fixed price dinner is served by candlelight in the intimate restaurant. *ETB* 👑 👑 👑, *AA***.

THE LAMB INN,
Shipton-Under-Wychwood,
Oxfordshire OX7 6DQ

Tel: 0993 830465

Accommodation (5 bedrooms, all with private bathroom); Free house; Historic interest; Dinners and snacks; Car park; Burford 4 miles.

As welcoming as the log fires which crackle a greeting during the winter months, the Lamb sits sedately on the outskirts of the village it has served well for many centuries now, and happily continues its long tradition of good hospitality and almost *smug* comfort. Guest rooms are individual in style, with colour television, clock radio and tea and coffee facilities — and while all are most pleasing to the eye it has been remembered that the most important item of furnishing is the bed itself. All here are supremely comfortable and ensure a good night's rest to all but the inveterate insomniac. Cuisine at the Lamb is on a par with the best of English country inns, with the finest local beef, lamb and poultry vying with fresh-caught fish and well-hung game on the menu. Service is friendly while retaining a simple courtesy, and the good wine list offers something for most tastes, pockets and occasions. In the bar, the fresh smell of furniture polish reminds one of yesteryear, and well-kept real ales provide the perfect accompaniment to substantial and varied bar food on offer, supplemented April to October by an outrageously tempting buffet.

THATCHED HOUSE HOTEL,
Manor Road, Sulgrave, Banbury, Oxfordshire OX17 2SE

Tel: 0295-76 232/262
Fax: 0295 712335

Accommodation (7 bedrooms, 5 with private bathroom); Historic interest; Luncheons and dinners; Car park (14); Silverstone 7 miles, Banbury 6.

This well-preserved seventeenth century building is situated in the tranquil village of Sulgrave, close to the borders of Oxfordshire, Northamptonshire and Buckinghamshire. Directly opposite the hotel is Sulgrave Manor, the ancestral home of George Washington, and there are many other historic houses and places of interest within easy reach. All the comfortable bedrooms, some with private bathrooms, are fully centrally heated, with colour television and tea-making facilities. The oak-beamed restaurant features country fresh foods, imaginatively prepared and complemented by a small but interesting wine list. The pleasant lounge and bar with its stone fireplace, together with the personal supervision of the owners, ensure a comfortable and relaxing stay. 🌷🌷🌷 *Approved.*

SPREAD EAGLE HOTEL,
Cornmarket, Thame, Oxfordshire OX9 2BW

Tel: 084421 3661
Fax: 0844 261380

Accommodation (22 bedrooms, all with private bathroom); Free house; Historic interest; Luncheons, dinners and snacks; Car park (80); Aylesbury 9 miles.

It was in the 1920s when the eccentric John Fothergill bought it that this sixteenth-century coaching inn found fame, for he antagonised his farming customers, stopped the regularly held masonic dinners and was downright rude to commercial travellers, creating for himself a new clientele composed of artists, academics and politicians, drawn by the rumours of his peculiarity as well as by the renown of his cooking. One of John's boasts was that he never used anything but the very finest of ingredients, and that habit has been maintained today in the restaurant which bears his name. Diners may choose from three separate menus — à la carte, table d'hôte and a special alternative which features mainly vegetarian dishes that go far beyond the usual few options open to this rapidly growing minority. Those seeking accommodation are well served, all comfortable and freshly decorated guestrooms being equipped with colour television, radio and telephone as well as having private bathroom. Two-night breaks are offered throughout the year and special packages which include a Garden-lovers Weekend (the famous Waterperry Gardens and Mattock's Roses are not far) and Antiques and History Weekend. 🌷🌷🌷🌷, ***.

Shropshire

Royal Oak
CARDINGTON

ROYAL OAK,
Cardington, Near Church Stretton,
Shropshire SY6 7JZ
Tel: 06943 266

Accommodation (one bedroom with private bathroom); Free house; Historic interest; Dinners and snacks; Church Stretton 4 miles.

Good, wholesome home-cooked food is the principal attraction of this most ancient of Shropshire hostelries ably run by the ever-obliging John and Sheila Seymour, who are renowned for their Shropshire Fidget Pie — and usually included on the menu are such favourites as steak and kidney or cottage pie, curry, chilli-con-carne and macaroni cheese. In the evenings a more comprehensive menu includes gammon and egg and substantial, flavoursome rump steaks. Accommodation is limited to one nicely-furnished double room with shower and toilet en suite, but those fortunate enough to have secured it will be delighted with the comfort it offers and the first class English breakfast which greets one on rising. The Royal Oak is located in a very pretty village set amongst beautiful walking country in the south Shropshire hills.

CROWN INN,
Hopton Wafers, Near Cleobury Mortimer, Shropshire DY14 0NB

Tel: 0299 270372
Fax: 0299 271127

Accommodation (8 bedrooms, all with private bathroom); Free house; Historic interest; Luncheons (not Saturday), dinners (not Sunday) and snacks; Car park (50); Cleobury Mortimer 2 miles.

We made the effort to ascend nearby Clee Hill and the views over Wales and the Welsh Marches were breathtaking as well. Where better, then, to refresh oneself than in this attractive old stone-built inn where comfort, good food and service as well as excellent overnight accommodation are there for the asking. The home-made dishes served mid-day and evening in the restaurant appear innovative and there was also a wide range of bar snacks on offer. If the weather is fine, refreshment may be taken on one of the two patios overlooking a lawn fringed by a stream. This is a lovely spot for a quiet country holiday and the inn provides well-furnished guest rooms, all of which have bathrooms en suite.

CHURCH INN,
The Buttercross, Ludlow, Shropshire SY8 1AW

Tel: 0584 872174

Accommodation (9 bedrooms, all with private bathroom); Free house; Historic interest; Luncheons, dinners and snacks; Worcester 29 miles, Leominster 11.

Centrally situated by the Buttercross of this ancient town, the Church Inn has had a variety of uses over the years, serving as the premises for barber-surgeon, saddler and druggist amongst others. Today, as well as providing a welcoming "local" it offers well appointed and comfortable overnight accommodation to the visitor, having nine en suite guestrooms complete with colour television and tea and coffee facilities. Guest beers are featured regularly in the bar, where a good selection of simple snacks and quite substantial meals may be obtained, and advice to book a table in the restaurant is evidence of its popularity. *AA Listed, Les Routiers recommended.*

TALBOT INN,
Much Wenlock,
Shropshire TF13 6AA

Tel: 0952 727077

Accommodation (6 bedrooms, all with private bathroom); Free house; Historic interest; Dinners and snacks; Car park (6); Bridgnorth 8 miles.

It has been known for travellers to stop off at the Talbot for a night en route to Wales and still be here a week later, for there is something about this fourteenth-century hostelry which makes one feel especially safe and at peace within its ancient walls. Guest bedrooms are in the converted malthouse in the courtyard, which also houses a comfortable residents' lounge and breakfast room, and all are attractively furnished and with private facilities. A good choice of home-cooked dishes is available lunchtime and evening, and even those on the strictest of diets should give in for once and sample the famous bread and butter pudding. 🌼🌼🌼 *Commended, Egon Ronay Grade 1 Accommodation, Good Pub Guide.*

Somerset

THE MALT SHOVEL INN,
Blackmoor Lane, Cannington,
Bridgwater, Somerset TA5 2NE

Tel: 0278 653432

Accommodation (4 bedrooms, one with private bathroom); Free house; Luncheons and dinners; Car park; Taunton 9 miles.

Those who follow the Malt Shovel signpost near Cannington on the A39 west of Bridgwater will be amply rewarded. In addition to well-kept real ale and a most cheering welcome from licensees Robert and Frances Beverley they will find a tempting array of reasonably priced bar food, ranging from a freshly cut sandwich to more substantial homemade pies, and succulent T-bone steaks. Comfortable bed and breakfast accommodation is available, and residents who would dine in style are recommended to the very good restaurant which attracts both local and passing trade. Children are welcomed.

GEORGE HOTEL,
Castle Cary,
Somerset BA7 7AH
Tel: 0963 50761

Accommodation (16 bedrooms, all with private bathroom or shower); Historic interest; Luncheons, dinners and snacks; Car park; Bath 25 miles, Longleat 19, Glastonbury 15, Stourhead 10.

This thatched, fifteenth century coaching inn has been tastefully modernised. All the cottage-style bedrooms have their own private facilities, including direct-dial telephone, radio and colour television. The elegant beamed restaurant offers a reasonably priced table d'hôte menu, and there is an extensive bar menu which increases the excellent food selection. The George bar is warmed by a roaring log fire in the original Inglenook fireplace, and is a popular meeting place for locals. The atmosphere in this privately run inn is warm and friendly, relaxing and stylish. Room rates include English Breakfast and VAT. Weekend and mid-week breaks are available all year. Visa, Access and Eurocard are accepted, as are children and dogs. The inn is situated in a rich area for sightseeing and touring and is ideal for visitors to the Bath and West Showground (3 miles), Wincanton National Hunt Racecourse (5 miles) and many National Trust properties and gardens. *ETB* 👑 👑 👑, *RAC **.*

THE WHITE HART,
Fore Street, Castle Cary,
Somerset BA7 7BQ
Tel: 0963 50255

Accommodation (3 bedrooms); Dinners and snacks; Car park (20); Weymouth 30 miles, Bristol 29, Weston-super-Mare 28, Bath 25.

This beautifully renovated old coaching inn dates back to the seventeenth century and today, under its welcoming hosts Charlie and Fiona Anderson, specialises in good home cooking. In such a convivial atmosphere relaxation comes easily, with lively chatter with the locals and unspoilt countryside to walk and enjoy within a stone's throw from the inn. Castle Cary is delightfully placed for half-day visits to numerous places of geographic and historic interest, with day excursions including the coast which may be reached by car within one hour. The inn has very comfortably appointed accommodation and the terms represent excellent value at £14 single, £25 double per night for Bed and Breakfast, with reductions for a stay of one week or more.

THE OLD PARSONAGE,
Barn Street, Crewkerne,
Somerset TA18 8BP
Tel: 0460 73516

Accommodation (10 bedrooms, all with private bathroom); Free house; Historic interest; Luncheons, dinners and snacks; Car park (11); Salisbury 51 miles, Dorchester 22, Lyme Regis 17.

It is in the quality of service, of personal attention, and in the provision of those special touches that the small family-run hotel scores every time over the larger establishment, and the Old Parsonage is a fine example of the former. Comfortable accommodation is in individually designed bedrooms, all complete with radio, colour television, telephone and hot drinks facilities, plus complimentary bath salts, shampoo and luxurious towels. The cheerful restaurant, warmed by a winter log fire, offers both table d'hôte and à la carte menus and enjoys an excellent reputation locally for fine cuisine. The Old Parsonage is ideally placed for visits to local National Trust properties and gardens.

EXMOOR WHITE HORSE INN,
Exford,
Somerset TA24 7PY

Tel: 064 383 229

Fax: 064 383 246

Accommodation (19 bedrooms, 18 with private bathroom); Free house; Historic interest; Dinners and snacks; Car park (40); Dunster 9 miles.

No one is quite sure just how old this prettily situated hostelry is — but there is little doubt that it has been sitting comfortably beside its stream for well over three hundred years. Almost all of the nineteen traditionally styled guestrooms have private facilities, and colour television, radio and tea trays are standard throughout. Service in the restaurant combines friendliness with professionalism, and a daily special is offered on a menu which features the most tender of veal in a cream sauce, local venison and fresh-caught lobster and trout, together with succulent grills and a carvery which enjoys a reputation far and wide.

THE GEORGE INN AT NUNNEY,
Church Street, Nunney, Near Frome,
Somerset BA11 4LW

Tel: 037-384 458/565

Accommodation (13 bedrooms, all with private bathroom); Free house; Historic interest; Luncheons, dinners and snacks; Beer garden; Car park; Bristol 27 miles, Bath 18, Wookey Hole 16, Wells 14, Frome 3.

Set in the picturesque village of Nunney, opposite the moated Norman castle, the fourteenth and seventeenth century George is a recommended touring headquarters. There is a great deal to see, including Longleat, the beautiful lake and gardens at Stourhead, the cathedral city of Wells, and Cheddar with its caves. Nevertheless, the inn has many attractions on its own account, not least of which is the reputation for providing excellent food. Meals and snacks are available at lunchtime and in the evening, together with real ale. Pets are welcome by arrangement. Comfortable accommodation is available in well-appointed rooms, all but one of which are en suite. Bargain breaks and weekly terms available throughout the year. *ETB* 👑 👑 👑, *AA **, Egon Ronay, Ashley Courtenay Recommended.*

NOTE

RALEGH'S CROSS INN,
Brendon Hills, Near Watchet,
Somerset TA23 0LN

Tel: 0984 40343

Accommodation (9 bedrooms, all with private bathroom); Free house; Historic interest; Lunches, dinners and snacks; Car park (200); Minehead 15 miles, Barnstaple 15, Exford 13.

The gateway to Exmoor National Park. Seasons display their changing moods and colours well upon this wild landscape, and this hospitable and cosy establishment 1250 feet above sea level makes an excellent vantage point. A bungalow annexe provides six comfortable en suite guest rooms to supplement the three in the original building, all tastefully furnished and with the added amenity of colour television. To ensure that it is a holiday for all concerned meals may be taken in the highly recommended restaurant of the inn, or in the snug bar where a wide range of freshly prepared starters, over 25 main courses cooked to order, and desserts are available to suit all tastes. There is a family room and an outside play area. Nearby attractions include Clatworthy Lake (3 miles) and Wimbleball Lake, a 374-acre reservoir which caters for a wide range of watersports.

WASHFORD INN,
Washford, Watchet,
Somerset TA23 0PP

Tel: 0984 40256

Accommodation (8 bedrooms, all with private bathroom); Free house; Bar meals; Car park (30); Bridgwater 15 miles.

Children are particularly well catered for at this pleasant country inn, having a separate play area within the lawned gardens and their own special menu. Adults too will find everything most satisfactory. Over fifty items are listed on the menu offered both lunchtime and evening, ranging from steaks and fish dishes to mouthwatering pies and pastries, and although food is usually served in the bar, a quiet dining room is available as an alternative eating venue. All guest bedrooms have en suite shower, colour television, tea and coffee facilities and telephone, and the recently renovated inn is centrally heated throughout. AA Listed.

EGREMONT HOTEL,
Fore Street, Williton,
Somerset TA4 4QQ

Tel: 0984 32500

Accommodation (9 bedrooms, 2 with private bathroom); Free house; Historic interest; Luncheons, dinners and snacks; Car park; Bridgwater 18 miles, Taunton 16.

Those who have three nights to spare will find value-for-money bargain break terms for bed, breakfast and evening meal at this welcoming old Somerset inn. Guest bedrooms here are spacious and comfortable, with a mix of traditional and modern furnishings, and some are available with private facilities. Public bar and lounge bar provide a choice of venue for refreshment, and good and varied bar meals are served during opening hours. More formal dining is to hand in the restaurant where the à la carte menu should amply satisfy all tastes. There is a beer garden and a function room for 100 people.

ROYAL OAK INN,
Withypool,
Somerset TA24 7QP

Tel: 064-383 506/7 Fax: 064-383 659

Accommodation (8 bedrooms, 6 with private bathroom); Free house; Historic interest; Dinners and snacks; Car park (20); London 194 miles, Exeter 37, Taunton 34.

Author R.D. Blackmore wrote his famous novel *Lorna Doone* while staying at the Royal Oak in 1866, and while it cannot promise to inspire such lasting prose today, it is indeed an inspiration to lovers of fine food and olde worlde graciousness. Individual furnishings give the guestrooms here character and charm, and all are fully equipped with tea and coffee facilities, hairdryer, colour television, radio and telephone. One may choose from à la carte or table d'hôte menus in the lavish restaurant which is open nightly, and a varied bar lunch and supper menu is offered in the snug comfort of the Rod Room Bar.

Wells Cathedral from the East.

Staffordshire

THREE HORSESHOES INN,
Blackshaw Moor, Leek,
Staffordshire ST13 8TW

Tel:053-834 296

Accommodation (6 bedrooms, all with private shower); Free house; Dinners and snacks; Car park (100); Derby 28 miles, Stafford 24, Stoke-on-Trent 11, Buxton 7.

This family-run inn is situated on the A53, approximately seven miles from Buxton, with breathtaking views of the Staffordshire Moorlands and the bizarre stone formation of The Roaches. Stone walls, oak beams and log fires give an olde worlde atmosphere. Fine traditional foods are served in the Carvery, while the restaurant offers à la carte and candlelit menus using fresh vegetables and local beef, poultry, game and cheeses, accompanied by a fine wine list. At weekends a well-attended dinner dance offers a fine choice of food, wine, music and dancing into the early hours. Accommodation is available in six cottage-style bedrooms, with showers, telephone, television and tea-making facilities. For relaxation in fine weather there are large gardens with patios, terraces and a children's play area.

PLEASE ENCLOSE A STAMPED
ADDRESSED ENVELOPE WHEN
WRITING TO ENQUIRE ABOUT
ACCOMMODATION FEATURED IN
THIS GUIDE

WHEATSHEAF INN AT ONNELEY,
Barhill Road, Onneley,
Staffordshire CW3 9QF

Tel: 0782 751581
0782 751499

Accommodation (9 bedrooms, all with private bathroom); Free house; Lunches (Sundays), dinners and snacks; Car park (150); Newcastle-under-Lyme 5 miles.

Situated on the main A525 between the villages of Madeley and Woore, just ten minutes from Newcastle-under-Lyme, this eighteenth-century family owned establishment faces south over the Staffordshire hills in an area of considerable natural beauty, and provides admirably for both businessman and tourist. Individually appointed guestrooms are furnished to the highest standard of comfort and all have private bathroom with hairdryers, colour television which offers satellite channels, tea and coffee facilities, radio, trouser press and telephone. A newspaper is provided daily and on arrival one finds the welcoming touch of a fruit basket. Good bar lunches and suppers are available, and in the evening an excellent dinner is served in the candlelit restaurant. *ETB* 👑 👑 👑, *AA**, RAC 2 Tankards.*

Suffolk

THE SEAFARER HOTEL,
Nethergate Street, Clare,
Suffolk CO10 8NP

Tel: 0787 277449

Accommodation (5 bedrooms); Children welcome, pets by arrangement; Car park (10); London 57 miles, Newmarket 16, Sudbury 9.

This extremely attractive small country hotel is pleasantly set in the beautiful large village of Clare. The Seafarer Hotel is centrally situated, one minute's walk from the much acclaimed Castle Country Park, with its Castle ruins, old railway station, and lake and river walks. It is also one minute's walk from the many shops and the market place. Only last year the Seafarer Hotel was awarded star ratings from both the RAC and AA (with an extremely high quality award), the Commended Award from the Tourist Board, and Les Routiers' award for the restaurant. The large garden, log fire and excellent bedrooms all make the Seafarer a favourite hotel. *ETB* 👑 👑 👑 *Commended, RAC Highly Acclaimed, AA *, Les Routiers.*

THE CROWN,
Market Hill, Framlingham,
Suffolk IP13 9AN

Tel: 0728 723521
Fax: 0728 724274

Accommodation (14 bedrooms, all with private bathroom); Free house; Historic interest; Luncheons, dinners and snacks; Car park (12); Woodbridge 9 miles.

The only thing not unique about the Crown is its name, for this is a true gem of an inn, dating back to the 1500s, overlooking the town from its vantage point on Market Hill. Colour television, tea and coffee facilities, radio and telephone are provided in all of the en suite guestrooms, many of which are furnished with genuine antiques. Additionally the hotel boasts a superior suite with lavish four-poster bed, which is perfect for any special occasion. Hot and cold food is served in the bar and lounge, and the pleasant surroundings of the restaurant are highly conducive to one's enjoyment of the cuisine. *RAC**, AA***.*

THE ANGEL,
Market Place, Lavenham,
Suffolk CO10 9QZ

Tel: 0787 247388

Accommodation (7 bedrooms, all en suite); Historic interest; Luncheons, dinners and snacks; Car park; London 65 miles, Harwich 21, Ipswich 19, Colchester 17, Stowmarket 15, Sudbury 7.

Visitors come from all over the world to this delightful old wool town with its beautifully preserved church, Guildhall and Tudor houses. Family run, The Angel overlooks the lovely market place and has been an inn since its first licence was granted in 1420. Although it has recently been fully refurbished, it retains a wealth of period features. The seven en suite bedrooms all have telephone, colour television and tea/coffee making facilities. The restaurant menu changes daily and features fresh local ingredients. In late spring and summer you can enjoy a selection of real ales in the courtyard or garden to accompany your food from the barbecue or cold table.

GEORGE AND DRAGON,
Hall Street, Long Melford, Sudbury,
Suffolk CO10 9JB

Tel: 0787 71285

Accommodation (7 bedrooms, one with private bathroom); Historic interest; Luncheons, dinners and snacks; Car park (14); Sudbury 3 miles.

Good cheer, good hospitality and good value are to be found at this attractive roadside inn, worth a visit whether one is seeking a comfortable bed for the night or simply sustenance and refreshment while breaking a journey. A varied bar menu is on offer throughout the year, and all food is freshly prepared on the premises with local produce used where possible. Summer barbecues are held regularly in the gardens, with one undercover pit to foil the British weather, and live entertainment is provided twice weekly. The village boasts the finest church in Suffolk, two Tudor halls open to the public and over thirty antique shops! 👑 👑, *1990 Good Beer Guide, Camra B&B Guide.*

COUNTRYMEN RESTAURANT AT THE BLACK LION HOTEL,
Long Melford,
Suffolk CO10 9DN

Tel: 0787 312356

Accommodation (10 bedrooms, all with private bathroom); Free house; Historic interest; Luncheons and dinners; Car park (10); Ipswich 24 miles, Colchester 18.

Ten spacious en suite bedrooms, each individually decorated and having only the facilities of television, telephone and tea and coffee trays in common, await the overnight visitor at this lovely old converted coaching inn which overlooks Long Melford's magnificent village green. All the thoughtful little touches of a privately owned, family-run establishment are obvious here — a veritable home-from-home where nothing is too much trouble. Added to this is a highly reputed restaurant serving delicious classic and modern English food, complemented by well-chosen and reasonably priced wines. Luncheon and dinner are served in the dining room with views of the nicely tended walled garden.

KING'S HEAD INN,
Front Street, Orford, Near Woodbridge,
Suffolk IP12 2LW

Tel: 0394 450 271

Accommodation (6 bedrooms); Free house; Historic interest; Luncheons (holidays and weekends), dinners (not Sunday or Thursday), snacks; Car park (40); Ipswich 20 miles.

If the ancient timbers of this former smugglers' haunt could talk there would doubtless be many a fascinating tale — but as they can't one must make do with the stories told by the locals who gather here of an evening. Good food is served in the bar as well as in the intimate and indeed rather elegant candlelit restaurant, where fresh locally-caught fish and lobsters and well hung game are specialities on a particularly pleasing menu. Guest accommodation is provided in charming olde-worlde bedrooms, and room rate includes an astonishingly good breakfast which at a small extra charge the indolent may partake of in bed. *AA, RAC, Egon Ronay, Good Pub Guide.*

THE CROWN,
High Street, Southwold,
Suffolk IP18 6DP

Tel: 0502 722275

Accommodation (12 bedrooms, all with private bathroom); Historic interest; Luncheons, dinners and snacks; Car park (24); Ipswich 35 miles, Lowestoft 13.

As charming and gracious as the old world town itself, this sturdy, well-run hotel offers overnight accommodation in twelve recently refurbished guest rooms, all of which are en suite and equipped with telephone and television. Even those who do not intend lingering in the area are recommended to the Crown for its excellent food. Morning coffee, afternoon tea and good bar meals are served daily, and a two or three course set luncheon and dinner menu is offered in the restaurant. Advice to book for the latter is evidence of its local popularity.

THE FOUR HORSESHOES,
Thornham Magna, Near Eye,
Suffolk IP23 7HD

Tel: 037-971 777

Accommodation (8 bedrooms, all with private bathroom); Free house; Historic interest; Luncheons, dinners and snacks; Car park (110); Norwich 24 miles.

In every sense the traditional thatched English inn of one's fondest imagination, the "Shoes" dates back to the 12th century. Its quaint beamed bars and restaurant, lovingly refurbished, recall the passing of the ages, but there is nothing archaic about the amenities provided in the beautifully appointed guest rooms, all of which have private bathrooms, colour television, direct-dial telephone and tea/coffee making facilities. The inn offers an extensive selection of bar meals, and the restaurant presents a full à la carte menu, with specialities including locally produced game, beef and sea food. Children are very welcome at concessionary rates. Delightfully placed in the tranquil Suffolk countryside, the "Shoes" provides the opportunity to savour luxurious facilities and true British hospitality in an historic setting.

Surrey

CROWN INN,
The Green, Chiddingfold,
Surrey GU8 4TX
Tel: 0428 682255

Accommodation (8 bedrooms, all with private bathroom); Free house; Historic interest; Luncheons, dinners and snacks; Car park; Milford 5 miles.

Built in 1258, this ancient hostelry is thought to have played host to Edward VI and Queen Elizabeth I, as well as the travelling pilgrims and Cistercian monks for whose shelter it was originally intended. Today's discerning traveller will find beautifully appointed guestrooms offering rest and overnight comfort, some with sumptuous four-poster beds, and all with television and traditional decor. Candlelight is reflected from the polished wood panelling of the restaurant where an extensive wine list complements quality cuisine, and the Huntsman Bar is a popular venue for lighter lunches and snacks. Traditional cream teas are served on the terrace, or, in inclement weather, in the cosy lounge.

THE WOOLPACK,
The Green, Elstead, Godalming
Surrey GU8 6HD
Tel: 0252 703106

No accommodation; Historic interest; Luncheons, dinners and snacks; Car park; Godalming 4 miles.

This very attractive tile-hung inn graces a quiet village not far removed from the urban practicalities of Farnham and Guildford. We found it to be extremely comfortably furnished with a large bar with beams and pillars giving it shape and character. At one end, we took note of a spruce restaurant where dishes, some of intriguing variety, are dispensed, between noon and 2 p.m. and 7 p.m. to 9.45 p.m. Ale is served straight from the cask. A family room leads to a garden with tables, children obviously being borne very much in mind judging from the provision of a swing and toys.

INN ON THE LAKE,
Godalming, Near Guildford,
Surrey GU7 1RH

Tel: 048-68 5575/6

Fax: 0483 860445

Accommodation (20 bedrooms, 18 with private bathroom); Free house; Historic interest; Luncheons, dinners and snacks; Car park (100); London 32 miles, Guildford 4.

Referring to this elegant establishment as an *inn* is rather like calling the QE2 a boat but that is what proprietors Martin and Joy Cummings insist on — for while service, accommodation and cuisine are definitely of country hotel standard, there is a spirit of informality and genuine cosiness here which follows all the great traditions of innkeeping. One gets the feeling that Martin and Joy and their carefully chosen staff actually *like* looking after their guests, in the same way one might enjoy entertaining a personal friend. Nothing is too much trouble — and yet all seems effortless and uncontrived. Guest bedrooms have been individually decorated in the style which seems best suited to each, and are provided with colour television, radio, tea tray, hairdryer and telephone. All have a luxuriously appointed en suite bathroom, and six executive rooms overlooking the lake have jacuzzi bathrooms. An atmosphere of grace and old-fashioned elegance pervades the restaurant where two good fixed price menus and an à la carte menu are offered with a most acceptable wine list, but those who choose to eat in the bar will find an array of tempting home-made dishes always available. This enchanting retreat is situated on the A3100 a little way south of Godalming and within easy reach of London and the south coast ports. ♛ ♛ ♛

THE WHITE HORSE,
Hascombe, Near Godalming,
Surrey
Tel: 048-632 258

No accommodation; Historic interest; Luncheons, dinners and snacks; Car park; Guildford 4 miles.

Motoring through leafy Surrey lanes, this attractive old village hostelry proved quite a find. In parts 400 years old and nestling in an area of outstanding rural beauty, the inn holds a special attraction for family parties, particularly in the summer, for it has a large garden with ample seating. Inside, in the pleasant bars, snacks of great variety were being dispensed and meals from the full à la carte menu in the restaurant were enthusiastically received. Prices represented excellent value. Within easy distance of Guildford and Horsham, the White Horse is the ideal focal point for a rewarding country drive.

THE SQUIRREL INN,
Hurtmore Road, Hurtmore, Near Godalming,
Surrey GU7 2RN
Tel: 0483 860223

Accommodation (7 bedrooms, all with private bathroom); Historic interest; Luncheons, dinners and snacks; Car park; Guildford 5 miles, Godalming 2.

This recently converted and refurbished country inn offers accommodation of an exceptionally high standard in imaginatively converted seventeenth century cottages. All rooms are en suite, and have tea/coffee making facilities, colour television, direct-dial telephone, automatic baby listening and alarm call. The luxuriously furnished bar and restaurant offers an excellent selection of real ales and fine wines, as well as a superb choice of home-cooked food, freshly prepared from the finest ingredients. There are many places of interest in this beautiful part of the English countryside, including Losely House, Charterhouse School and the Devil's Punchbowl. This is a family-run establishment, offering a very high level of hospitality and service. *Relais Routiers.*

East Sussex

STAR INN,
Alfriston,
East Sussex BN26 5TA

Tel: 0323 870495
Fax: 0323 870922

Accommodation (34 bedrooms, all with private bathroom); Free house; Historic interest; Luncheons, dinners and snacks; Car park (40); London 60 miles, Eastbourne 9.

Although the Star has its roots in the thirteenth century much of the present building dates from the mid-fifteenth and many features of that time have been beautifully preserved. Visitors wishing overnight accommodation may choose from traditionally furnished inn rooms or the modern, up-to-the-minute bedrooms of the new wing, safe in the knowledge that whichever they opt for, comfort is assured and colour television, radio, tea and coffee facilities and telephone are supplied. All of course are en suite. In the olde-worlde restaurant, heavily timbered as is the bar, à la carte and daily changing table d'hôte menus offer a pleasing and well planned selection of dishes. *AA and RAC ***.*

SWAN INN,
Woods Corner, Dallington,
East Sussex TN21 9LB

Tel: 042-482 242

Accommodation (3 bedrooms); Free house; Historic interest; Luncheons, dinners and snacks; Car park; Heathfield 5 miles.

Enjoying an elevated position in this area designated as one of outstanding natural beauty, the Swan, a fourteenth century coaching inn, offers splendid views of the south coast, stretching as far as Beachy Head on a clear day. Accommodation here is limited and reasonably priced, and one is advised to book early to be sure of a room. Daily changes are rung on the bar menu which features mostly wholesome homemade fare such as beef stew with dumplings, chicken, ham and mushroom pie, and some good vegetarian specials. Do leave room, though, for one of the delicious old-fashioned puddings available. A flower-filled garden is set with tables in summer, and provides a pleasant spot for al fresco drinks.

GUN INN,
Gun Hill, Horam, Heathfield,
East Sussex TN21 0JU

Tel: 0825 872361

Accommodation; Luncheons, dinners and snacks; Car park; Heathfield 3 miles.

Tucked away in the heart of picturesque Sussex countryside, the Gun Inn is somewhat hard to find but with the aid of a map and a penchant for exploration, the effort will prove to be well worth while. Hosts Roy and Joy Brockway run this pleasant retreat and present an excellent and extensive bar food menu at lunchtime and in the evening. A fine place for a tranquil holiday away from it all or as a touring port of call, the Gun has well-appointed guest rooms, one of which has a bathroom en suite, and the terms for accommodation are reasonable indeed.

THE ROSE AND CROWN INN,
Fletching Street, Mayfield,
East Sussex TN20 6TE

Tel: 0435 872200

Accommodation (3 bedrooms, all with private facilities); Free house; Historic interest; Luncheons, dinners and snacks; Car park; Tunbridge Wells 8 miles.

Set in the historic village of Mayfield, this lovely old inn has been used by wayfarers and travellers on the road between London and the coast for the last 500 years. And its flower-laden frontage is still a welcome sight for weary travellers in the south of England. Bedrooms are well appointed, and accommodation is reasonably priced. Bar meals can be enjoyed in the garden or in any of the four bars, and restaurant meals are available throughout the day and evening. The Rose and Crown is in every pub guide available and has been star awarded in the Egon Ronay guide since 1981. Many places of historic interest lie within easy reach.

West Sussex

SWAN HOTEL,
High Street, Arundel,
West Sussex BN18 9AG

Tel: 0903 882314

Accommodation (13 bedrooms, all with private bathroom); Free house; Historic interest; Luncheons, dinners and snacks; Car park; London 56 miles, Worthing 10.

In this wholesome establishment fresh locally caught fish, superb quality meats delivered daily and flavoursome vegetables straight from the good earth transport one back to an age before the tinned, frozen and prepacked took over to dull the tastebuds. Food here is the real thing, whether served in the grander surroundings of the restaurant or partaken informally in the bar where soft music is a bonus, not an intrusion. Continuing the traditional values, en suite bedrooms are spotlessly clean and supremely comfortable, all having tea-making facilities, colour television and telephone. Most major credit cards are accepted. 👑 👑 👑

JACK AND JILL INN,
Brighton Road, Clayton,
West Sussex

Tel: 079 18 3595

Accommodation (3 bedrooms); Luncheons, dinners and snacks; Car park (80); Brighton 6 miles.

This nursery rhyme pub seven miles north of Brighton on the A273 finds special favour with families, for youngsters are made most welcome here and provided with playground and their own children's room. Tea-making facilities are standard in all three guestrooms, which are bright and cheerful-looking with whitewood furniture and pleasing decor. Regular attention keeps them spotlessly clean, as are the two shower rooms they share. Good bar food is served both at lunchtime and in the evenings, and hosts Mike and Joan Harman personally attend to their guests' every comfort.

ELSTED INN,
Elsted, Near Midhurst,
West Sussex

Tel: 073-081 3662

No accommodation; Free house; Historic interest; Dinners and snacks; Midhurst 3 miles.

Another masterpiece for real ale enthusiasts, this pleasant Victorian-style inn stocks the complete range of Ballards beers, which are brewed in a nearby village. Other good beers are also available in company with wholesome bar fare, served until 10p.m. Excellent, simple, locally produced food is offered at reasonable prices, always with something to suit vegetarians and the younger members of the family. This is an unpretentious and friendly place well worth a recommendation. At the rear is a large garden with tables scattered amongst the fruit trees, a delightful spot in which to refresh oneself on summer days and at very reasonable prices. A room is set aside for families.

THE BLACK HORSE,
Nuthurst, Horsham,
West Sussex

Tel: 0403 891272

No accommodation; Free house; Historic interest; Snacks; Car park (30); Horsham 3 miles.

Once upon a time, this attractive inn was part of a row of old cottages. Now it is a spruce and well-kept hostelry with great care taken to preserve its rural ambience. The bars are warmly welcoming aided by the retention of the low-beamed ceilings, stone-slab floors and huge open fire. It was sunny when we called and we took good refreshment on a patio overlooking a charming garden in company with a sizeable number of other, obviously satisfied, customers. Food is served every day.

LION HOTEL,
Nyetimber Lane, Pagham, Bognor Regis,
West Sussex PO21 3JX

Tel: 0243 262149

Accommodation; Free house; Historic interest; Luncheons, dinners and snacks; Car park; Chichester 7 miles, Bognor Regis 5.

It is easy to imagine Nyetimber as the smuggling village it once was. Tucked away in a lonely corner of the Sussex coast between Bognor and Pagham, the situation for its nefarious purposes would have been ideal. The early fifteenth century "Lion" was heavily involved in these practices and, standing in the low-beamed bars today, one can easily transport the mind to these romantic days. Now an attractive country inn, fronted by a patio with sun umbrellas where refreshment may be taken, the old inn offers traditional hospitality with excellent à la carte luncheons and dinners. Snacks are available in the bar.

STAR INN,
130 High Street, Steyning,
West Sussex BH44 3RD

Tel: 0903 813078

No accommodation; Historic interest; Snacks; Shoreham-by-Sea 5 miles.

Once upon a time, this 18th century village inn was a home for waifs and strays run by the Quakers. It is a far happier picture today for tourists and locals seeking refreshment are the only ones to stray into its welcoming atmosphere. The bar, with its beamed ceiling, is a congenial place in which to enjoy good food, attractively served, backed up by good ale, several guest beers always being available on tap. On cool days, a log fire adds to the overall comfort. Outside, there is a charming paved and lawned area adjacent to the village stream, safely separated from children by a fence. *Ploughman's Lunch Award; Wine and Spirit Educational Trust Certificate, Garden and Fascia Competition Runner-up.*

Tyne and Wear

THE ORIGINAL MASONS,
Hexham Road, Walbottle,
Tyne and Wear

Tel: 091-267 5563

No accommodation; Free house; Historic interest; Luncheons, dinners and snacks; Car park (46); Newcastle 5 miles.

Those searching for a traditional English pub, with no blaring television set or noisy pub games, need look no further than this friendly establishment, only three minutes from the A69. First granted its liquor licence in 1796, it has recently been completely refurbished, with no expense spared to provide comfortable seating and beautiful furnishings. The excellent restaurant offers a tempting à la carte menu, with a choice of dishes ranging from traditional English to some with an international flavour. A wide range of bar snacks is also offered, and parents will be pleased to note that there is a special children's menu. The Original Masons is only a short drive from the city of Newcastle, and there are interesting Roman ruins nearby which are well worth a visit. *Les Routiers, Good Food Guide.*

PLEASE ENCLOSE A STAMPED ADDRESSED ENVELOPE WHEN WRITING TO ENQUIRE ABOUT ACCOMMODATION FEATURED IN THIS GUIDE

Warwickshire

WHITE HORSE INN,
Ettington, Near Stratford-upon-Avon,
Warwickshire
Tel: 0789 740641

Accommodation (4 bedrooms, some with private bathroom); Historic interest; Luncheons, dinners and snacks; Car park (30); London 87 miles, Oxford 34, Birmingham 30, Stratford-upon-Avon 6.

What could be more delightful for a holiday or short break in Shakespeare country than a stop-over in this lovely old inn, already conjuring up the atmosphere of days gone by with its furnishings, oak beams, and the warmth of its welcome. Guests can enjoy a glass of real ale with their lunch, and for those who choose to stay longer, the Inn's restaurant serves fine fare in the evening. There is a sun patio and beer garden in which to take advantage of warmer weather. The White Horse's accommodation means that tired visitors may take full advantage of its location, six miles from Stratford and close to Warwick Castle and the Cotswolds. Also near to NEC Birmingham and the Royal Showground at Stoneleigh. All rooms are comfortably furnished (en suite available), with washbasins, radiators, colour television and tea/coffee making facilities. Proprietors Roy and Val Blower. *ETB* 👑 👑.

NOTE

All the information in this book is given in good faith in the belief that it is correct. However, the publishers cannot guarantee the facts given in these pages, neither are they responsible for changes in policy, ownership or terms that may take place after the date of going to press. Readers should always satisfy themselves that the facilities they require are available and that the terms, if quoted, still apply.

HALFORD BRIDGE INN,
Fosseway, Halford, Shipston-on-Stour,
Warwickshire CV36 5BN

Tel: 0789 740382

Accommodation (5 bedrooms, 3 with showers); Historic interest; Luncheons, dinners and snacks; Car park (40); Banbury 12 miles, Stratford-upon-Avon 8.

On the principle that you can't have too much of a good thing Tony and Greta Westwood, proprietors of this charming sixteenth century inn, keep their kitchens open seven days a week to provide sustenance to regulars, residents and hungry passers-by. A wide range of good hot and cold bar food is available, in addition to the excellent fare offered at reasonable prices in the restaurant. Good home cooking is the speciality here, with home-made pickles, sauces, pies etc, as well as fresh vegetables whenever possible. All the comfortably furnished bedrooms have colour television, and tourists who must keep an eye on their budgets as well as the scenery will find them good value for money. *ETB* ♛ ♛, *Egon Ronay, Les Routiers, AA Recommended.*

West Midlands

SALTWELLS INN,
Saltwells, Brierley Hill,
West Midlands DY5 1AX

Tel: 0384 69224

Accommodation (13 bedrooms, 8 with private bathroom); Free house; Snacks; Car park (100); Dudley 2 miles.

There are few people who don't look twice at the bar menu in Alan and Gill Stewart's splendid hostelry, for the prices seem so low one fears having misread them. Meals are available all day and food here is good and plentiful, with a choice of dishes as varied as one could wish. Children are welcome; swings and a chute are provided for them in the tree-bordered garden which is floodlit at night. Visitors seeking accommodation within the Saltwells Nature Reserve will find comfortably furnished single, twin and double en suite rooms, all with colour television and beverage-making facilities. Access and Visa are accepted.

WHITTINGTON INN,
Kinver, Near Stourbridge,
West Midlands DY7 6NY

Tel: 0384 872110

No accommodation; Free house; Historic interest; Luncheons, dinners and snacks; Car park (300); Birmingham 16 miles, Kidderminster 4.

The history of this ancient manor house is as interesting and varied as the menus now presented here, and visitors who would follow its changing fortunes are recommended to the comprehensive guide which is available. Decor and furnishings throughout the inn are not only traditional but original, fostering the feeling that one has stepped back in time to a more gracious age. The same atmosphere of elegance is continued in the restaurant where an à la carte menu offers Italian cuisine. Less formal fare is available seven days a week in any of the bars, also in the Bistro upstairs. The menu has a wide selection of home cooked hot and cold foods.

Wiltshire

THE BEAR HOTEL,
Devizes,
Wiltshire SN10 1HS

Tel: 0380 722444

Accommodation (25 bedrooms, all with private bathroom); Historic interest; Luncheons, dinners and snacks; Car park, garages; London 86 miles, Salisbury 25, Warminster 15, Marlborough 14.

This old coaching inn has a fascinating history dating back from the sixteenth century, and at one time was the home of Sir Thomas Lawrence, the portrait painter. The Bear has always been a hive of activity and has an impressive list of famous patrons including King George III. Today, the excellent hotel attracts visitors by reason of its first-rate accommodation and cuisine. Well-modernised guest rooms all have private bath facilities, colour television, radio and telephone. There are two restaurants and a tempting selection of bar food. The inn is within easy reach of a host of interesting places. 👑 👑 👑 👑, *AA****, *Egon Ronay*.

THE BECKFORD ARMS,
Fonthill Gifford, Tisbury, Salisbury,
Wiltshire SP3 6PX

Tel: 0747 870385

Accommodation (7 bedrooms, all with private bathroom); Historic interest; Dinners and snacks; Car park (40); Shaftesbury 7 miles.

The charming eighteenth century Beckford Arms lies in fine rolling countryside in an area of outstanding natural beauty. Easily reached are the Cathedral city of Salisbury, the seaside town of Bournemouth, Bath, Stonehenge, Longleat, Stourhead Gardens and other places of interest. The Beckford Arms boasts seven tastefully furnished bedrooms, all with modern facilities including en suite bathrooms, colour television etc. Some have four-poster beds. Friendly bars and restaurant provide log fires, real ales, good food and fine wines. It is conveniently situated two miles from Tisbury station and the A303. Special breaks available. ♛ ♛ ♛, *CAMRA "Beer, Bed and Breakfast".*

THE WHITE HART AT FORD,
Ford, Near Chippenham,
Wiltshire SN14 8RP

Tel: 0249 782213

Accommodation (11 bedrooms, all with private bathroom); Free house; Historic interest; Dinners and snacks; Car park (100); London 104 miles, Bristol 17, Bath 13, Chippenham 5.

If there were a competition for the most idyllically situated inn, the White Hart at Ford would surely be among the favourite contenders. This centuries-old, stone-built pub with its wealth of beams, log fires and solid old world charm rests beside a trout stream which meanders through the surrounding meadow and looks serenely over the lush Weavern Valley. Luxurious four-poster rooms are included in the guest accommodation at this delightful retreat, and all rooms are thoughtfully provided with colour television, radio, and tea-making facilities, as well as having bathroom en suite. Cuisine, like accommodation, is of first rate standard, and meals may be taken in either the renowned Riverside Restaurant or in the popular Buttery. Gardens are carefully tended and feature a swimming pool along with secluded terraces for sunbathing or quiet meditation.

ROYAL OAK INN,
Great Wishford, Near Salisbury,
Wiltshire SP2 0PD

Tel: 0722 790229

Accommodation; Historic interest; Luncheons, dinners and snacks; Car park; Salisbury 8 miles, Wilton 3.

Just a short drive from Salisbury, the Royal Oak is set in a lovely village just off the A36. The kitchens are open seven days a week offering an unusually comprehensive menu to cover most possibilities for regulars, residents and hungry passers-by. Chilli, curry, moussaka, lasagne, burgers, omelettes and an interesting choice of steaks are just a few examples of the home-made meals available. Children are most welcome and can choose either children's portions (where practicable) or from a special menu.

RED LION INN,
Kilmington, Warminster,
Wiltshire BA12 6RP

Tel: 09853 263

Accommodation (2 bedrooms); Free house; Historic interest; Snacks; Car park (25); Mere 4 miles.

Even if not planning to linger in the area, it is worth a detour to sample the hospitality of this four-hundred-year-old tavern. The Red Lion has retained its traditional character, with two log fires, delightful period furniture including a curved settle and, most importantly, NO juke box or gaming machines! Bar food is largely home-made, with a tempting selection of modestly priced toasties, open sandwiches and filled baked potatoes. Delicious ploughman's lunches and salads and a daily selection of hot dishes are also available, with even more choice in the evenings (except Monday and Tuesday). Proprietor Chris Gibbs is renowned locally for the excellent condition of his beers, and takes pride in offering a wide selection of keg and real ales, ciders and lagers. Those tempted to linger in this delightful area can find comfortable overnight accommodation in an attractive double or twin room. Local attractions include the National Trust property of Stourhead Gardens and House, as well as Longleat Safari Park and many delightful unspoilt villages. For the more energetic, White Sheet Hill behind the inn and Stourhead Woods offer lovely walks.

NETTLETON ARMS,
Nettleton, Chippenham,
Wiltshire SN14 7NP

Tel: 0249 782783

Accommodation (4 bedrooms, all with private bathroom); Free house; Historic interest; Luncheons (Sundays only), dinners (Wed.–Sat.) and snacks; Car park (50); Chippenham 7 miles.

Once the manorhouse of the Codrington family, this early sixteenth-century establishment still has the air of a cherished private residence with its fine furnishings, polished wood, minstrels' gallery and well-tended log fire. Overnight guests are accommodated in the converted medieval barn, once used by monks as a school for young gentlemen, and all en suite bedrooms are exceedingly well appointed and decorated in attractive fashion. Quality bar lunches and suppers are served, with a menu which is extensive enough to provide for all tastes.

OLD BELL INN,
2 Saint Ann Street, Salisbury,
Wiltshire SP1 2DN

Tel: 0722 27958

Accommodation (7 bedrooms, all with private bathroom); Free house; Snacks; Car park; Southampton 23 miles, Amesbury 8.

The fourteenth and twentieth centuries meet well at this enchanting hostelry – the former offering old timber beams, huge log fires and medieval atmosphere, the latter providing the comfort of full central heating and spacious guest rooms with en suite facilities. Double and twin rooms are available, and two especially charming rooms have stately four-poster beds. The Old Bell stands adjacent to Salisbury Cathedral, offering extensive views of the Cathedral Close and conveniently situated for all the amenities of the town. Lunch is served in the bar between 12.30 and 2.00pm, when a good range of hot and cold dishes is offered.

OLD BELL HOTEL,
Market Place, Warminster,
Wiltshire BA12 9AN

Tel: 0985 216611

Fax: 0985 217111

Accommodation (24 bedrooms, 15 with private bathroom); Historic interest; Luncheons, dinners and snacks; Car park (20); Salisbury 20 miles, Bath 16.

The Old Bell looks very much as it did at the time the nineteenth-century social reformer William Cobbett visited Warminster and described it as a town "full of everything that is solid and good". Today his description is just as apt, and one of the best and most solid attractions of the one-time great corn-marketing centre is this charming colonnaded establishment. Guest bedrooms are individual in style and decor — most having bathroom en suite and all being equipped with colour television, radio, telephone and tea and coffee facilities — and room rates include a substantial English breakfast with home-made jams and marmalade, and also a morning newspaper. An assortment of home-made snacks is available each lunchtime in the Olde Worlde Bar, where the welcome is as warm as the crackling log fire which burns throughout the winter, or alternatively one may choose from the cold table in Chimes Bar, partaking of one's favourite dish, perhaps, in the sweet-smelling flowered courtyard when the weather permits. Timberwork and exposed beams probably dating back to the old Bell Inn of the 1480s grace the restaurant, open every lunchtime and evening for good à la carte meals served by candlelight, and on Sunday for a traditional luncheon roast. **

ROYAL OAK,
Wootton Rivers, Near Marlborough,
Wiltshire SN8 4NQ
Tel: 0672 810322

Accommodation (6 bedrooms, 2 with private bathroom); Free house; Historic interest; Luncheons, dinners and snacks; Car park (35); Pewsey 3 miles.

One feature of this charming sixteenth-century thatched inn which overnight visitors find particularly welcome is an 'open kitchen' where one may help oneself to breakfast whenever it is required. Other meals may be partaken formally in the restaurant or in the cheerful surroundings of the bar where light snacks as well as more substantial dishes are served at lunchtime and in the evening. Guest accommodation comprises twin, double and single rooms, some with private bathroom, and decor throughout the inn is fresh and appealing. If Wootton River Lock seems vaguely familiar, it may be that one has seen it in that popular TV series 'The River'.

Worcestershire

LITTLE PACK HORSE,
High Street, Bewdley,
Worcestershire DY12 2DH
Tel: 0299 403762

No accommodation; Free house; Historic interest; Luncheons, dinners and snacks; Kidderminster 3 miles.

A traditional little neighbourhood pub with ancient black beams and flagstone floors and with rooms bedecked with old photographs, this interesting inn is well worth tracking down. It stands just off the High Street, the oldest pub in a charming old Midlands town; it dispenses boundless hospitality and freshly cooked fare (from Rump Steak to Desperate Dan Pie!) and excellent real ales including its own brew, the now famous Lumphammer bitter — as potent as it sounds! There is a relaxed, friendly atmosphere with no aggravating background music or bright lights. Children are welcome, families being accommodated in the former stable block complete with items of tack. *Mercury Food Awards, CAMRA Beer Award.*

CHEQUERS INN,
Chequers Lane, Fladbury, Pershore,
Worcestershire WR10 2PZ

Tel: 0386 860276

Accommodation (8 bedrooms, all with private bathroom); Free house; Historic interest;
Luncheons, dinners and snacks; Car park (30); Evesham 3 miles.

A perfect example of the traditional English hostelry, the Chequers Inn stands at the end of a quiet lane in this delightful village in the Vale of Evesham. Those seeking accommodation will find beautifully kept en suite guestrooms, individually furnished and decorated, some with balconies, some with open rural views, and all well equipped with every modern facility, including television, radio, telephone and tea trays. Even if time precludes one staying a while in this charmed area, the Chequers is still worth a flying visit for its fine fare. A carvery is provided Thursday, Friday and Saturday evenings and Sunday lunchtime, while bar meals and an à la carte menu are available daily except on Sunday evening when it is residents only. *ETB* 👑 👑 👑 *Approved.*

THE HADLEY BOWLING GREEN INN,
Hadley Heath, Near Droitwich,
Worcestershire WR9 0AR

Tel: 0905 620294

Accommodation (14 bedrooms, all with private bathroom); Free house; Historic interest;
Dinners and snacks; Car park (80); Droitwich 3 miles.

This historic 15th century inn is situated in the heart of Worcestershire, yet only 10 minutes from the M5 motorway. The bowling green itself is one of the oldest in Britain, and was played on by many of the leading Elizabethan nobility. All bedrooms have private bath/shower and toilet, colour television, direct-dial telephone, hairdryer, trouser press and tea/coffee making facilities. Some have four-posters; three cottage-style rooms across the courtyard are ideal for those who prefer ground floor accommodation. An extensive à la carte menu is offered in the intimate dining room and a comprehensive bar snack menu is available in the two delightful bars, which also feature a wide choice of beers. You will find a friendly, relaxed atmosphere at the Hadley Bowling Green Inn, which is convenient for Worcester and Droitwich and only 30 minutes' drive from the NEC and Birmingham Airport.

THREE KINGS INN,
Hanley Castle, Worcester,
Worcestershire WR8 0BL

Tel: 06846 2686

Accommodation (one bedroom with private bathroom); Free house; Historic interest; Snacks;
Tewkesbury 8 miles, Worcester 8, Malvern 5.

Not far from the River Severn, this little fifteenth century free house just off the B4211 is well worth taking the trouble to find. The cosy bar and comfortable oak-beamed lounge contain a wealth of "old world" features — inglenook fireplaces where log fires blaze in the winter months, winged settles, bake ovens, and a fascinating collection of old domestic and agricultural objects. The inn has been run by the same family since 1911, and you are assured of a friendly welcome and personal service. Grills and hot and cold snacks are prepared to order both lunchtimes and evenings, except on Sunday evenings, when live entertainment is provided. Traditional ales are served, and a private room is available for small parties.

WHITE LION HOTEL,
Upton-upon-Severn,
Worcestershire WR8 0HJ
Tel: 06846 2551

Accommodation (10 bedrooms, all with private bathroom); Free house; Historic interest; Luncheons, dinners and snacks; Car park (20); Tewkesbury 6 miles.

Part of the novel *Tom Jones* was set here and the Wild Goose and Rose Rooms, both mentioned in Fielding's famous work, have been beautifully preserved, the latter with a magnificent four-poster bed to provide the ultimate in cossetting. The Rose Room, like all other guest bedrooms in this fine establishment, is equipped with colour television, radio alarm and direct-dial telephone, and of course has a well-fitted private bathroom. Room price includes early morning tea as well as a full English breakfast, and other meals may be taken as desired in the charming, oak-beamed Burgundy Restaurant or comfortable and informal lounge bar. ♕ ♕ ♕ ♕, *AA and RAC ***; Signpost, Johansens and Ashley Courtenay Recommended.*

North Yorkshire

KING'S ARMS HOTEL AND RESTAURANT,
Market Place, Askrigg in Wensleydale,
North Yorkshire DL8 3HQ
Tel: 0969 50258 Fax: 0969 50635

Accommodation (10 bedrooms, all with private bathroom); Free house; Historic interest; Dinners and snacks; Car park (20); Ripon 20 miles, Richmond 11.

"The perfect Herriot setting" featured in the BBC series "All Creatures Great and Small". This ancient, listed coaching inn, noted for its immense character, atmosphere, comfort and good food, faces the famous TV vet's house across the Market Square of Askrigg. There are three unique bars, with inglenook fireplace, log fires, panelled walls and original saddle hooks. The ten bedrooms are all en suite, with colour television and tea/coffee making facilities. Some rooms have antique poster/canopy beds. The restaurant serves the finest English cuisine, home-cooked using local produce and game in season. Bar meals are available lunchtimes and evenings. Guests are assured of a warm welcome and personal attention all the year. Come and savour the peace and beauty of the Dales; linger awhile and discover the special magic of the North. *AA**, RAC**, Ashley Courtenay, Egon Ronay, Les Routiers, Johansens, Good Hotel and Good Pub Guide, CAMRA, Good Beer Guide.*

SHIP INN,
Acaster Malbis, York,
North Yorkshire YO2 1XB

Tel: 0904 705609 and 703888

Accommodation (8 bedrooms, all with private facilities); Free house; Historic interest; Luncheons, dinners and snacks; Car park (30); Leeds 17 miles, York 3.

A really picturesque holiday retreat on the banks of the Yorkshire Ouse, this attractive and well-run hostelry is yet only a short distance from the magnificence of York, the United Kingdom's second most popular tourist attraction. Offering first-class fare and spruce accommodation, including one four-poster bedroom and a family room, the inn makes a superb holiday headquarters and is equally popular with boating enthusiasts and businessmen. Excellent evening dinners are served in the relaxed atmosphere of the old-world restaurant, whilst a wide range of lunches and evening snacks may be enjoyed in the friendly Riverside Bar, adjacent to which is a garden where children may disport themselves in summer. Those with a penchant for fishing may be well accommodated and the inn has its own moorings for residents and visitors. Further afield, the Yorkshire Dales beckon and the coast may be reached in less than an hour.

ROSE AND CROWN HOTEL,
Bainbridge, Wensleydale,
North Yorkshire DL8 3EE

Tel: 0969 50225

Accommodation (12 bedrooms, all with private bathroom); Free house; Historic interest; Dinners and snacks; Car park (65); Ripon 31 miles, Richmond 23, Hawes 4.

One of the nicest of the Wensleydale villages with its classic green and beautiful old stone houses, Bainbridge is a worthy setting for this most picturesque hotel, which was dispensing hospitality and cheer long before Henry VIII came to the throne. Today all of the twelve guest bedrooms have the luxury of private facilities, colour television, tea/coffee makers, clock radios and hair dryers. Good local produce is used extensively in the spotless kitchens, and tempting, skilfully prepared dishes are served in the large, pleasant dining room overlooking the village green, as well as less formally in the snug bars. ♔ ♔ ♔, *AA and RAC **, Egon Ronay, Johansen, Ashley Courtenay, Good Food Guide.*

BUCK INN,
Buckden, Upper Wharfedale, Near Skipton,
North Yorkshire BD23 5JA   Tel: 075676 227/228/352

Accommodation (15 bedrooms, all with private bathroom); Free house; Historic interest; Dinners and snacks; Car park (30); Kettlewell 4 miles.

Proprietors Trevor and Phoebe Illingworth describe their solid Georgian hostelry as an inn for all seasons and one cannot really dispute that, for whether one samples its hospitality on a festive Christmas or New Year break or spring weekend or summer retreat, one immediately feels thoroughly at home and at peace here. Bedrooms have private facilities, colour television, tea and coffee facilities and telephone, and are delightfully furnished in cottage style as well as being supremely comfortable. Cuisine is as pleasing as accommodation, and fresh local produce features well on the extensive menus offered in both restaurant and cosy old-world bar. *ETB* 👑 👑 👑 👑*, AA and RAC**.*

NEW INN,
Clapham, Near Settle,
North Yorkshire LA2 8HH   Tel: 046-85 203 Fax: 496

Accommodation (13 bedrooms, all with private bathroom); Free house; Historic interest; Dinners and snacks; Kendal 21 miles, Skipton 21.

Keith and Barbara Mannion invite you to their friendly eighteenth century residential coaching inn in the picturesque Dales village of Clapham. Ideal centre for walking the three peaks of Ingleborough, Pen-y-ghent and Whernside. All rooms have full en suite facilities, colour television and tea/coffee facilities. Enjoy good wholesome Yorkshire food in our restaurant, or bar meals in either of our two bars. Dogs welcome. Ring Barbara for full details. *ETB* 👑 👑 👑*, Member of Wayfarer Inns.*

DEVONSHIRE ARMS,
Cracoe, Skipton,
North Yorkshire BD23 6LA   Tel: 0756 73237

Accommodation (3 bedrooms); Dinners and snacks; Car park (100); Grassington 3 miles.

Neat herbaceous borders flank the terrace of this traditional Dales pub and create a pleasant spot for a meal or a drink when the weather is fine. Bar fare, carefully prepared to order on the premises, is served from noon until two throughout the week and from 6.45 until 9.30 every evening but Monday, and includes some more unusual offerings in addition to the ever popular steak and kidney or chicken and mushroom pies, sausage and mash and ploughman's. Dinner may be taken in the restaurant Tuesday to Saturday, and those wishing overnight accommodation will find well-appointed double and twin rooms, all with tea and coffee facilities.

WHITE LION INN,
Cray, Buckden, Near Skipton,
North Yorkshire BD23 5JB

Tel: 075-676 262

Accommodation (5 bedrooms, all with private shower); Historic interest; Luncheons, dinners and snacks; Car park; Leeds 40 miles, Skipton 18, Hawes 9.

Nestling beneath Buckden Pike at the head of Wharfedale, the White Lion Inn has been tastefully restored to offer five en suite bedrooms, while retaining its original beams, open log fires and stone-flagged floors. Traditional English fare is served in the bar or cosy dining room; children's menu available. The Inn provides a good choice of beers and spirits, including traditional hand-pulled ales, which in fine weather can be enjoyed in the beer garden. Parents can relax while children enjoy themselves in safety in the enclosed play area. The Inn is on the path of many recognised walks in the very heart of the Yorkshire Dales and makes an ideal base for touring and walking. The thriving market town of Skipton and Aysgarth with its famous falls are both less than half an hour away. There are also many sporting activities locally, including pony trekking, rock climbing, pot holing and golf. Pets welcome if well-behaved. Open all year.

HORSESHOE HOTEL,
Egton Bridge, Near Whitby,
North Yorkshire

Tel: 0947 85245

Accommodation (6 bedrooms, 3 with private bathroom); Free house; Historic interest; Luncheons, dinners and snacks; Car park (40); Whitby 7 miles.

A solidly built and most appealing old inn run by David and Judith Mullins, the Horse Shoe stands peacefully on the River Esk amid the North Yorkshire Moors National Park but just seven miles from Whitby and the attractions of the many holiday towns and villages on this charming coast. Local produce features well on the nicely varied menu (changed weekly) which is presented in the dining room and a range of tasty snacks is available at all times in a snug bar with open fire. En suite accommodation awaits the overnight guest and rooms are well furnished and comfortable.

TEMPEST ARMS HOTEL AND RESTAURANT,
Elsack, Skipton,
North Yorkshire BD23 3AY
Tel: 0282 842450

Accommodation (10 bedrooms, all with private bathroom); Luncheons, dinners and snacks; Free house; Historic interest; Car park; Skipton 4 miles.

It is perhaps disconcerting to think that the French can teach the English something about running a good Yorkshire pub, but there are many who could take lessons from Francis Boulongie, the licensee of this most inviting of country inns which flies the tricolour alongside the English flag. Generous helpings of delicious home-cooked food are served in the bar from noon until 2.15 and again from 6.30 until 10.00 p.m. Traditional French onion soup and fish soup feature on the choice of starters, and main meals include a wonderful seafood platter as well as the long established pub favourites like grilled gammon with fried egg, steak, kidney and mushroom pie and liver and onions. More formal culinary demands are catered for in the restaurant, open every day for luncheon and dinner chosen from varied table d'hôte menus. These change regularly and might offer such delicacies as salmon and halibut *en papillotte*, or black peppered sirloin steak flamed in brandy and served with a smooth cream sauce. Those seeking a cosy billet in this area will appreciate the new purpose-built accommodation, which comprises ten bedrooms all with full bath and shower facilities en suite, telephone and television.

THE NEW INN MOTEL,
Main Street, Huby, York,
North Yorkshire YO6 1HQ

Tel: 0347 810219

Accommodation (8 chalets, all en suite, with shower); Historic interest; Dinners and snacks; Car park; York 9 miles.

Nine miles north of York, in the village of Huby in the Vale of York, the Motel is an ideal base for a couple of nights away to visit York (15 minutes to nearest long-stay car park), or a longer stay to visit the East Coast of Yorkshire, the Dales, the Yorkshire Moors, Herriot Country, Harrogate and Ripon. The Motel is situated behind the New Inn (a separate business), which, contrary to its name, is a 500-year-old hostelry, originally an old coaching inn, and full of character. All chalets are en suite (singles, doubles, twins and family rooms) and have colour television and tea-making facilities. Good home cooking is served, including vegetarian meals, and full English breakfast is a speciality. Pets are welcome. The accommodation is suitable for the disabled. Licensed.

THE FORRESTERS ARMS,
Kilburn, Near Thirsk,
North Yorkshire YO6 4AH

Tel: 03476 386

Accommodation (8 bedrooms, all with private bathroom); Free house; Historic interest; Luncheons, dinners and snacks; Thirsk 6 miles.

Right in the heart of James Herriot country, within the North Yorkshire National Park and next door to the world famous workshops of Robert Thompson (the "Mouseman" who carves a tiny mouse on every piece of furniture he makes), this twelfth century inn has much to recommend it as a base for those who wish to tour this part of Yorkshire. Each guest feels more like a family friend than a visitor, and the ample and well presented Yorkshire fare will more than satisfy the heartiest appetite. Real ale is available in the cheerful bar and visitors may drop in for morning coffee, bar lunch or evening meal. *ETB* ♛ ♛ ♛ ♛, *RAC* **.

Please mention
Recommended WAYSIDE INNS
when seeking refreshment or
accommodation at a Hotel
mentioned in these pages

WHITE SWAN,
Market Place, Pickering,
North Yorkshire YO18 7AA

Tel: 0751 72288

Accommodation (13 bedrooms, all with private bathroom); Free house; Historic interest; Luncheons (Sunday), dinners and snacks; Car park (25); Whitby 20 miles, Scarborough 16, Malton 8.

If the extensive wine list at this charming old hotel daunts one, please do seek the advice of helpful proprietors Ken and Deirdre Buchanan, for both are connoisseurs and Deirdre herself is a *Dame de la Jurade de Saint Emilion*. Worthy of the fine cellar is the Swan's daily changing menu, and good local produce combines beautifully with the chef's skill and artistry to create a cuisine which is truly memorable. Bar food too is available at lunchtime and a well-stocked gantry ensures most reasonable demands can be met. All guest rooms have en suite facilities, tea and coffee trays and colour television, and the exquisite Ryedale Suite provides for those seeking that extra touch of luxury. 🦢🦢🦢🦢, *AA and RAC**.*

THE GEORGE HOTEL,
Piercebridge, Darlington,
North Yorkshire DL2 3SW

Tel: 0325 374576

Accommodation (35 bedrooms, all with private bathroom); Free house; Historic interest; Luncheons, dinners and snacks; Car park (200); Darlington 5 miles.

Dick Turpin is reputed to have been a regular caller at The George Hotel, which was formerly a coaching inn. Piercebridge was the site of a Roman fort and is on the Roman road called Dere Street (now the B6275 leading to the A68). The George is situated on the banks of the River Tees, which is on the border between Yorkshire and Durham, making it an ideal base for exploring Herriot Country, the Yorkshire Dales, Moors and North East Coast. The riverside gardens and walks are a must for nature lovers with regular sightings of kingfishers and herons. There is also good fishing here. All rooms have en suite bathroom, colour television, radio alarm, hospitality tray, central heating and direct-dial telephone. The menu in the delightful restaurant overlooking the river offers a wide range of interesting dishes, complemented by a fine wine list. There is a very comfortable residents' lounge. **

THE OLD DEANERY RESTAURANT,
Minster Road, Ripon,
North Yorkshire HG4 1QS

Tel: 0765 3518

Licensed; 2 bedrooms, one en suite and one with private bathroom; Car park (50); Harrogate 11 miles.

Those who are fortunate enough to stay at this former Dean of Ripon's residence will appreciate the relaxing atmosphere and personal attention of their hosts. Set in one-and-a-half acres of wooded grounds, and opposite Ripon Cathedral, it is ideally placed for touring the Dales and North Yorkshire Moors. The restaurant has an excellent reputation for its cuisine and also offers a full vegetarian menu.

FOXHOUND INN,
Flixton, Scarborough,
North Yorkshire

Tel: 0723 890301

No accommodation; Free house; Luncheons, dinners and snacks; Scarborough 9 miles, Filey 6.

This one-time humble country inn has been skilfully modernised to provide three spacious and delightfully decorated bars, and a restaurant that has already acquired a fine reputation for its cuisine and service. Holidaymakers from Scarborough, Filey and Bridlington are recommended to acquaint themselves with the pleasures offered by this cheerful and charming hostelry.

THE BUCK INN,
Thornton Watlass, Near Bedale, Ripon,
North Yorkshire HG4 4AH

Tel: 0677 22461

Accommodation (6 bedrooms, all with private bathroom); Free house; Luncheons, dinners and snacks; Car park (25); Ripon 11 miles, Northallerton 9.

Friendly country inn overlooking the delightful cricket green in a peaceful village just five minutes away from the A1. Newly refurbished bedrooms, all with en suite facilities, ensure that a stay at the Buck is both comfortable and relaxing. Delicious freshly cooked bar meals are served lunchtimes and evenings in the cosy bar and dining area. On Sundays a traditional roast with Yorkshire pudding is on the menu. Excellent Theakston and Tetley cask beer is available. This is an ideal centre for exploring Herriot country. There is a children's playground in the secluded beer garden where quoits are also played. ♛ ♛ ♛ *Approved, AA *.*

Publisher's Note

When you are booking ahead, please ask for written confirmation, including price and whatever else is included. If you have to cancel, give as long written notice as possible. Your booking is a form of contract and both the proprietor and yourself have obligations as a result.

It is important that you raise any complaints on the spot. In the unlikely event of a serious complaint not being settled to your satisfaction, you should let us know and we will follow it up. We cannot accept responsibility for the details of the published descriptions or for errors or omissions, but we are obviously anxious that you should enjoy whatever use you make of our entries and that the high standards are maintained.

THE WENSLEYDALE HEIFER,
West Witton, Leyburn,
North Yorkshire DL8 4LS
Tel: 0969 22322 Fax: 0969 24183

*Accommodation (20 bedrooms, all with private bathroom); Free house; Historic interest;
Luncheons, dinners and snacks; Car park: Richmond 8 miles.*

Yorkshire hospitality is famed the world over for its warmth and generosity, and you will not find a better example of true Yorkshire welcome than at The Wensleydale Heifer, set in the heart of Wensleydale and on the road to the Lakes. A charming example of a well-preserved inn — its seventeenth century character only enhanced by the addition of modern amenities — and run by Major and Mrs Sharp to offer unashamed comfort and pleasure in the most elegant surroundings, including oak beams, antique furniture, log fires and even a four-poster bed! Naturally there is a fine table with individually cooked dishes chosen from an extensive and seasonally varying à la carte menu complemented by an excellent cellar. Traditional Yorkshire Sunday lunches are most popular, as is the Bistro Bar with inexpensive home cooked and varied meals available lunchtimes and evenings seven days a week. *ETB* 👑 👑 👑 👑 *Commended, AA and RAC **, Egon Ronay, Michelin, Les Routiers, Johansens.*

South Yorkshire

THE RAMBLER INN,
Edale, Sheffield,
South Yorkshire S30 2ZA
Tel: 0433 70268

Accommodation (some rooms en suite); Meals and packed lunches; Car park; Matlock 20 miles.

An attractive stone-built hotel, the Rambler Inn is an ideal centre for cycling, mountaineering, walking and all outdoor pursuit holidays. It is situated close to the railway station and is set in its own grounds with ample car parking. Single, double or family rooms are available, all with tea/coffee making facilities. Most have colour television and some have en suite bathrooms. There is also attractive cottage accommodation within the grounds. Good wholesome food is available throughout the day, and packed lunches can be prepared if required. The hotel is fully licensed. The Peak District National Park offers a wealth of opportunities for all kinds of outdoor activities amidst magnificent scenery. The Inn is close to the start of the Pennine Way, the first of Britain's long-distance footpaths.

West Yorkshire

ROYAL HOTEL,
High Street, Boston Spa,
Yorkshire (West) LS23 7AY

Tel: 0937 842142

Accommodation (13 bedrooms, 12 with private bathroom); Historic interest; Luncheons, dinners and snacks; Car park (50); Doncaster 30 miles, Leeds 20, York 13.

Catering for the family and the businessman without sacrificing the needs of one to the other, this gracious old coaching inn looks thoroughly at home in the picturesque village of Boston Spa, just a mile from the A1 and well positioned halfway between York and Harrogate. Its thirteen bedrooms (12 en suite) are furnished with stylish good taste and the guest is provided with colour television, radio, telephone, beverage-making facilities and trouser press. Cuisine is of a standard comparable with accommodation, with hearty Yorkshire breakfasts, varied bar lunches and an excellent evening menu. The Carvery Restaurant is open every lunchtime and evening. Special weekend packages are offered.

OLD SILENT INN,
Stanbury, Near Haworth,
West Yorkshire

Tel: 0535 42503

Accommodation (12 bedrooms, all with private bathroom, including four-poster bedroom and Bridal Suite); Free house; Historic interest; Luncheons, dinners and snacks; Car park; Haworth 1 mile.

With a reputation for its homely atmosphere, good wholesome fare and comfortable accommodation, this cosy little free house stands close to High Withins, the "Wuthering Heights" of Emily Bronte's famous story. Bonnie Prince Charlie is reputed to have taken refuge at the 18th century inn during his flight from England and the locals were forbidden to mention the fact — hence the hostelry's quaint name. The most generous luncheons and à la carte meals are served, and home-made sweets. Bar meals are available daily and a carvery operates at Sunday lunchtimes. Prices for food and accommodation represent excellent value. Open all day, every day.

Clwyd

THE HAWK AND BUCKLE INN,
Llanefydd, Near Denbigh,
Clwyd LL16 5ED

Tel: 074-579 249

Accommodation (10 bedrooms, all with private bathroom); Free house; Historic interest; Dinners and snacks; Car park (20); Colwyn Bay 7 miles.

Every twentieth-century comfort is to be found at this welcoming village inn of the 1600s, clinging to the slopes of the Denbigh Hills and offering panoramic views over the Vale of Clwyd. All ten en suite guest rooms in the tasteful extensions are equipped with telephone, tea/coffee making facilities and television; trouser press and hair dryer available. Furnishings are comfortable and pleasing to the eye. Local game, pork, lamb and the freshest of freshly-caught salmon and trout are imaginatively served in the Hawk and Buckle's popular restaurant, and varied and substantial bar snacks are offered at lunchtime. Hosts Robert and Barbara Pearson will happily supply a wealth of information on the area. Visa and Access are accepted.

WYNNSTAY INN,
Llansilin,
Clwyd SY10 7QB

Tel: 069-170 355

Accommodation (5 bedrooms); Luncheons (Sunday), dinners and snacks; Car park (40); Llangollen 10 miles.

The village of Llansilin is set in picturesque countryside which is ideal for walking, fishing, pony trekking and bird watching. Wynnstay Inn is a family run hotel, offering comfortable accommodation and a warm, friendly welcome. There is a lounge with colour television; also central heating and log fires. Good wholesome food is served, ranging from bar snacks to à la carte meals.

WEST ARMS HOTEL,
Llanarmon D.C., Near Llangollen,
Clwyd LL20 7LD

Tel: 069-176 665

Fax: 069-176 262

Accommodation (14 bedrooms, all with private bathroom); Free house; Historic interest; Luncheons (Sunday), dinners and snacks; Car park; Llangollen 7 miles.

Recently refurbished to a high standard, this establishment remains as charming and unpretentious in atmosphere as in the days when it was a simple country inn. Comfort is the keynote here, and guest bedrooms are designed and fitted with that very much in mind. Delightfully decorated, all have their own private facilities, and two spacious suites also provide guests with an attractive sitting room. Public areas are well furnished and inviting, and log fires burn companionably in the grates to supplement the central heating on chillier days. Dinner at the West Arms is a pleasant, leisurely affair, with table d'hôte menus intentionally limited in order to preserve quality but nevertheless providing something for most tastes. Changed daily, some typical main courses might include breast of chicken with wild mushroom and sherry sauce, escalope of salmon with fresh lime, or succulent fillet steak, but any special requirement should be discreetly mentioned in advance and all reasonable steps will be taken to ensure that it is met. Those actively inclined will find the area offers some most invigorating walks, and pony trekking and fishing can be arranged. Three good golf courses lie within half an hour's drive of the hotel. *AA and RAC**, Johansen's Recommended Inns, Welsh Rarebits, Signpost, Ashley Courtenay.*

Dyfed

GOLDEN GROVE ARMS,
Llanarthney, Near Llandeilo,
Dyfed SA32 8JU

Tel: 0558 668551

Accommodation (8 bedrooms, 3 with private bathroom); Free house; Historic interest; Luncheons, dinners and snacks; Car park (120); Llandeilo 6 miles.

Fine food, friendly service and good hospitality combine in this attractive free house situated on the B4300. Comfortably furnished and well-appointed guest rooms, some with private facilities, are on hand to serve those desiring overnight rest, and the fine restaurant menu features several Welsh specialities. A nicely varied range of freshly prepared dishes is also available in the bar, and in warmer weather tables and chairs on terrace and lawn provide a pleasant venue for partaking of a snack and refreshment. Those in the bar on Friday or Saturday evenings can usually expect to be entertained with jazz, classical or modern music.

THE TREWERN ARMS,
Nevern, Near Newport, Dyfed

Tel: 0239 820395

Accommodation (10 bedrooms, all with private bathroom); Free house; Historic interest; Dinners and snacks; Car park (70); Newport 2 miles.

"Only a friendly country inn" is how proprietress Molly Sanders describes this homely establishment, but we must protest at the word "only" which suggests that a friendly country inn could somehow be found wanting! This is indeed a charming place, run by charming people. Black pepper steaks served on a Boar's Head platter is the speciality of the four-course restaurant, and an excellent selection of bar meals is served from 12 – 2pm and from 6 – 9pm. Nevern itself is a tiny village within the lovely Pembrokeshire National Park.

MARINERS INN,
Nolton Haven, Near Haverfordwest, Dyfed SA62 3NH

Tel: 0437 710469

Accommodation (11 bedrooms, all with private facilities); Free house; Historic interest; Luncheons, dinners and snacks; Car park (100); Haverfordwest 8 miles, St. Davids 8.

Mariners is an attractive, friendly, residential inn, standing only 40 yards from the sandy cove of Nolton Haven in Pembrokeshire National Park. It offers a fine base for exploring this lovely part of Wales. Bedrooms are well-appointed, all with satellite television, radio, room call, tea/coffee making equipment and private facilities. There is a large selection of bar meals. Table d'hôte and à la carte menus are served daily in the 1749 Smugglers Inn Restaurant, as well as traditional Sunday lunches. The Mariners is open all year. *WTB* 👑 👑 👑, *AA and RAC ** , Les Routiers, CAMRA.*

THE ROYAL OAK INN,
Rhandirmwyn, Llandovery,
Dyfed SA20 0NY

Tel: 055-06 201

Accommodation (5 bedrooms, 3 with private bathroom); Free house; Luncheons, dinners and snacks; Car park (25); Llandovery 6 miles.

"Free and Easy" can sometimes be synonymous with slapdash and badly run, but one need have no such fears at the Royal Oak. The proprietors here have managed to combine informality with efficiency, and friendliness with courteous good service. Spacious rooms offer comfort as well as attractive decor and most have colour television and private facilities. The very full menu presented in the restaurant caters for most tastes, and bar snacks are available together with a nice range of local beers. Dinner is from 6.00 until 10.30pm, and sleepyheads will be pleased to note that breakfast will be served right up till 10 in the morning.

Gwynedd

YE OLDE BULL'S HEAD,
Castle Street, Beaumaris, Anglesey,
Gwynedd LL58 8AP

Tel: 0248 810329
Fax: 0248 811294

Accommodation (11 bedrooms, all with private bathroom); Free house; Historic interest; Luncheons (Sunday), dinners and snacks; Car park (12); Caernarfon 12 miles, Holyhead 2.

Charles Dickens was one of the better known guests of this solid fifteenth-century inn, and characters from his novels are used to name the beautifully appointed en suite bedrooms all of which are graced with remote control colour television, radio and direct-dial telephone. Booking for the restaurant is strongly advised, an indication of the popularity it enjoys in the area, and an excellent wine list is a fitting complement to the first class cuisine. Locals and visitors to the town mingle well in the comfortable bar, warmed by log fire when there is a chill in the air and displaying a fine array of antique weaponry. *WTB* 🌸🌸🌸🌸 *with Merit.*

Dyfed/Gwynedd 137

WHITE HORSE INN,
Capel Garmon, Llanrwst,
Gwynedd LL26 0RW

Tel: 069-02 271

Accommodation (6 bedrooms, all with private bathroom); Free house; Historic interest; Dinners and snacks; Car park; Llanrwst 4 miles.

With its cheerful log fires, beamed ceilings and friendly atmosphere, this attractive sixteenth century free house is full of character. Its situation in one of the most scenic parts of Wales, coupled with the fine facilities offered by hosts Sandy and Malcolm McDonald, makes this a recommended port of call on a touring holiday. Indeed, one could do no better than stay here for a few days to enjoy first-class cooking, good company and comfortable accommodation. Modern appointments mix easily with old-world ambience. The little village of Capel Garmon stands high on the mountainside with superb views of Snowdonia.

YE OLDE BULL INN,
Llanbedr-Y-Cennin, Conwy,
Gwynedd LL32 8JB

Tel: 049-269 508

Accommodation (1 bedroom); Free house; Historic interest; Luncheons, dinners and snacks; Car park (40); Shrewsbury 83 miles, Barmouth 8, Conwy 5.

One need venture no further than the terrace of this sixteenth century inn to enjoy the splendours of Welsh scenery, for the views of the Vale of Conwy and mountains beyond are truly delightful from here. Overnight accommodation is homely, comfortable and modestly priced, as good value as the bar food which ranges from a toasted sandwich or jacket potato to prime steaks served with the appropriate accompaniments. An extensive menu is also to be found in the dining room, with its beams salvaged from a wrecked ship of the Armada. The bar too is beamed, and log fires, antiques and brassware add much to the atmosphere. Here on Sunday nights one is left in no doubt that Wales is the Land of Song.

PLAS YR EIFL HOTEL,
Trefor, Caernarfon,
Gwynedd

Tel: 0286 86 781

Accommodation (6 bedrooms, 3 with private bathroom); Free house; Historic interest; Dinners and snacks; Car park; Caernarfon 12 miles.

Happily trapped between sea and mountains, this family-run hotel built from local granite in 1890 has many attractions, not least of which is the friendly, relaxed atmosphere which makes one feel thoroughly at home and content. Two bars offer a choice of venue to partake of refreshment, one overlooking the sea as does the pretty dining room, where an extensive and daily changing menu makes good use of Neptune's bounty. Nicely furnished en suite guest rooms have colour television and tea and coffee facilities, and are individual in style and decor. Many popular resorts are easily reached from here by road, or one might take to the water in the hotel's own private power boat. *WTB ▲ ▲ ▲, Johansens.*

Powys

LION HOTEL,
Broad Street, Builth Wells,
Powys LD2 3DT

Tel: 0982 553670

Accommodation (20 bedrooms, 15 with private bathroom); Free house; Historic interest; Luncheons, dinners and snacks; Car park (14); Hereford 40 miles, Brecon 16.

Those with a minimum of two nights to spend are offered special rates at this solid and welcoming hotel by the river, and bedrooms (most of which have private bathroom) are equipped with colour television, telephone and facilities for making tea and coffee. A comprehensive range of quality fare is available here, from snacks at the bar to a good table d'hôte dinner or Sunday luncheon in the spacious restaurant, and picnics can be prepared for those who wish to travel further afield for the day. Service is courteous and obliging and private car parking is available. *WTB ▲ ▲ ▲.*

BULL HOTEL,
Presteigne,
Powys LD8 2BP

Tel: 0544 267488

Accommodation (6 bedrooms, all with private shower); Free house; Historic interest; Luncheons, dinners and snacks; Rhayader 26 miles, Hereford 23, Builth Wells 21, Ludlow 16, Knighton 6.

In a pleasant town in the beautiful Border countryside, the Bull Hotel is an excellent centre for walking, touring, fishing, golfing and pony trekking. All rooms have shower, television and tea/coffee making facilities. Some are en suite and one has a four-poster bed. Full à la carte menu. Special rates for stays of more than four nights; no charge for children under four years. Dogs welcome.

TRETOWER COURT INN,
Tretower, Near Crickhowell,
Powys NP8 1RF

Tel: 0874 730204

Accommodation (7 bedrooms, 2 with private shower); Historic interest; Luncheons, dinners and snacks; Car park (80); Abergavenny 6 miles.

Easily found on the A479, this appealing and picturesue pub-in-the-garden makes a most acceptable base from which to tour some of the lesser known corners of Wales. Comfortable bed and breakfast accommodation is provided in double, single and family rooms; single and double rooms have private showers. The lounge and public bars have a welcoming and convivial atmosphere, and the attractively decorated restaurant caters well for all tastes. Most of the present building dates from the seventeenth century, though the original inn on the site goes back a further 300 years.

Argyll

CAIRNDOW STAGECOACH INN,
Cairndow,
Argyll PA26 8BN

Tel: 04996 286/252

Accommodation (12 bedrooms, 10 with shower and toilet); Free house; Historic interest; Dinners and bar meals; Car park; Edinburgh 90 miles, Glasgow 48, Dunoon 29, Arrochar 12, Inveraray 10.

Amidst the beautiful scenery which characterises the upper reaches of Loch Fyne, this historic stagecoach inn enjoys a spectacular sheltered position. The stables have recently been transformed into a delightful restaurant, full of old world charm. Here one may dine well by candlelight from the table d'hôte and à la carte menus. There is also a new functions bar and games room. Bedrooms are fitted out comfortably, with electric blankets, radio, telephone, baby listening, and tea/coffee making facilities; most have a view of the loch. Some rooms have television and there is a residents' TV lounge. This is an ideal spot for touring Oban, the Western Highlands, Glencoe, the Trossachs, the Cowal Peninsula, Kintyre and Campbeltown. The inn is under the personal supervision of hosts Mr and Mrs Douglas Fraser, and the area offers fine opportunities for many outdoor pursuits and visits to famous beauty spots. Lochside beer garden, exercise room, sauna and solarium.

EASDALE INN/INSHAIG PARK HOTEL,
Easdale, By Oban,
Argyll PA34 4RF

Tel: 08523 256

Accommodation (7 bedrooms, 4 with private bathroom); Free house; Dinners and snacks; Car park; Oban 16 miles.

The famous eighteenth century Bridge over the Atlantic takes one onto Seil Island and this comfortable Victorian hotel, set in its own grounds overlooking the sea and the scattered islands of the Inner Hebrides. Otters can be seen regularly, as well as seals, badgers, deer and a varied birdlife. The special charm of this family-run establishment is reflected in the quality of service and the interest taken in each guest. Fresh local seafood is a speciality in the dining room, together with a wide range of beautifully prepared dishes. Twin, double, four-poster and superior twin rooms are available, all with colour television and most with private bathroom, and a good Scottish breakfast is included in the accommodation charge. Well mannered dogs are welcome at a small charge. *AA, RAC, Tourist Board Commended.*

CLACHAIG INN GLENCOE

Sue Scullard

CLACHAIG INN (Dept FHG),
Glencoe,
Argyll PA39 4HX

Tel: 08552 252

Accommodation (19 bedrooms, 16 with private facilities); Free house; Historic interest; Dinners and snacks; Car park (50); Glasgow 90 miles, Oban 41, Fort William 18.

Clachaig Inn is set amidst the magnificent mountains of historic Glencoe with fabulous views. Under family management this ancient drovers' inn continues the tradition of a warm and friendly welcome and the best of Highland hospitality. With en suite bedrooms and Scottish home cooking, Clachaig is the perfect base from which to tour, sightsee and savour the atmosphere so special to the West Coast. Clachaig is also an ideal base for the more energetic, be it for walking, climbing, sailing, cycling, photography or bird watching. After a pleasant day out and a delicious home-cooked meal, where better to relax than in our friendly bars with a selection of real ales and a choice of some 50 of the finest malt whiskies. Self-catering chalets also available. *Good Beer Guide.*

Berwickshire

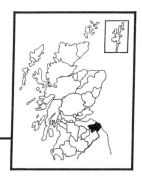

MITCHELL'S HOTEL,
West End, Chirnside,
Berwickshire

Tel: 089-081 507

Accommodation (4 bedrooms); Free house; Dinners and snacks; Car park; Berwick-upon-Tweed 7 miles, Duns 6.

Take the B6355 west from the A1 at Ayton and you will find yourself at this solidly built hotel, ably run by the Pollard family with the help of their chef Ronnie. The spacious, nicely laid-out bar boasts an extensive menu which will cater for most tastes, though for more formal dining there is always the option of a good à la carte menu in the locally popular dining room. Accommodation is comfortable and well appointed, rooms having television, tea/coffee facilities and washbasins. A sauna and sunbed are now available, as well as a large functions room. An ideal centre for golfing, fishing and shooting holidays. Stately homes, castles, coastline and the capital city are all within easy reach.

WHEATSHEAF HOTEL,
Swinton,
Berwickshire TD11 3JJ

Tel: 089-086 257

Accommodation (3 bedrooms); Free house; Dinners and snacks (not Mondays); Edinburgh 45 miles, Berwick-upon-Tweed 12.

First class bar food is the principal attraction of this appealing little hotel on the green, with fish dishes and fresh local produce a speciality of the extensive menu which also includes such delights as beef and Guinness pie, some good curries and crepes and lasagne. Do leave room for a pudding, however, as the list is a temptation to the strongest-willed. Those who would dine more formally are well served in the popular à la carte restaurant, and if overnight accommodation is sought three comfortable guest rooms are available with colour television, tea facilities and washbasins. Residents may use their own private lounge as well as bar and conservatory. *1990 Good Pub Guide "Food Discovery of the Year", Good Food Guide.*

Dunbartonshire

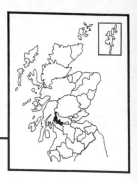

INVERBEG INN,
Near Luss, Loch Lomond,
Dunbartonshire G83 8PD

Tel: 043-686 678
Fax: 043-686 645

Accommodation (14 bedrooms, 7 with private bathroom); Free house; Historic interest; Dinners and snacks; Car park (80); Luss 3 miles.

It is difficult to believe one is only forty minutes from Glasgow at this one-time drovers' haunt on the west shore of Loch Lomond, for dramatic Highland scenery surrounds the lovely white-washed inn. Though traditional in character and appearance, all modern comforts are offered here and guest accommodation is pleasingly decorated with matching fabrics and tasteful colour schemes. Good food is available in restaurant and lounge bar, and one need not be tied to particular times, for meals may be partaken at any hour, a useful point for those wishing to explore the area either by road or by the ferry which plies from the inn jetty.

Edinburgh & Lothians

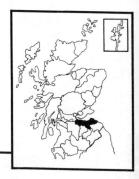

SUN INN,
Lothianbridge, Near Dalkeith,
Midlothian EH22 4TR

Tel: 031-663 2456

Accommodation (5 bedrooms, all with private bathroom); Free house; Historic interest; Luncheons, dinners and snacks; Car park; Edinburgh 12 miles.

With its origins in the late 1700s, this warmly welcoming family-run establishment is set in over five acres of enchanting garden and woodland on the River South Esk. Last year saw the completion of a bedroom development and now those who are drawn to the Sun by its fine value-for-money restaurant can be accommodated overnight in guest rooms appointed to real nineties-standard comfort. A varied menu has something for all tastes, with home-made puff pastry pies of chicken and mushroom, steak or smoked haddock, and a selection of curries, grills, chicken and fish dishes including a quite delectable trout in whisky and mushroom sauce. *Johansen's Guide to Country Inns, Pubs of Taste in Scotland.*

OLD ORIGINAL ROSLIN INN,
4 Main Street, Roslin,
Midlothian EH25 9LE

Tel: 031-440 2384

Accommodation (6 bedrooms, all with private bathroom); Free house; Historic interest; Luncheons, dinners and snacks; Car park; Loanhead 2 miles.

The Old Original was in former times a temperance hotel, but those seeking liquid refreshment may be assured that today all four bars are well stocked with good beers, spirits and a most acceptable selection of fine wines. Substantial lunches and suppers are served in the comfortable lounge, and the à la carte menu attracts locals, as well as residents and passing trade, to the well laid out diningroom which is graced by an interesting collection of antiques. Six bedrooms are available for letting, including a special honeymoon room, and all have pleasing decor, duvets and central heating.

HAWES INN,
Newhalls Road, South Queensferry,
West Lothian

Tel: 031-331 1990

Accommodation (8 bedrooms); Historic interest; Luncheons and dinners; Car park; Edinburgh 9 miles, Dunfermline 8.

The plot for the famous R.L. Stevenson novel *Kidnapped* was formulated in a room in this sixteenth-century establishment which overlooks the graceful Forth road and rail bridges. Today guests of literary leanings or otherwise will find accommodation in tastefully furnished bedrooms, all with tea-making facilities, and one with a rather grand four-poster bed. Cuisine of the finest standard is offered in the quality diner, and good bar lunches and basket suppers are served. Most of the major credit cards are accepted.

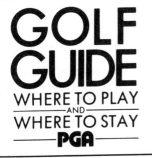

Available from most bookshops, the 1991 edition of THE GOLF GUIDE covers details of every UK golf course – well over 2000 entries – for holiday or business golf. Hundreds of hotel entries offer convenient accommodation, accompanying details of the courses – the 'pro', par score, length etc. *Old Thorns Golf Course & Hotel, Hampshire, features on the front cover with golfing editorial from the Professional Golfers' Association who also endorse the guide.* **£5.99 from bookshops or £6.50 including postage from FHG Publications, Abbey Mill Business Centre, Paisley PA1 1JN.**

Fife

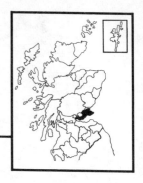

FOREST HILLS HOTEL,
Auchtermuchty,
Fife KY14 7AP

Tel: 0337 28318
Fax: 0337 57329

Accommodation (10 bedrooms, 7 with private bathroom); Free house; Historic interest; Luncheons, dinners and snacks; Edinburgh 29 miles, St. Andrews 16, Perth 15.

This traditional inn is situated in the square of the former Royal Burgh of Auchtermuchty, once a busy weaving centre. There are many places of historic interest nearby, as well as ample opportunities for sporting activities such as golfing, fishing, sailing, gliding and pony trekking. The hotel provides all the comforts the traveller expects, all bedrooms having colour television, tea/coffee making facilities, hair dryer and trouser press. Simple but appetising country fare, complemented by an interesting wine list, is served in the intimate bistro. Afterwards guests can relax in the comfortable surroundings of the lounge, or in the charming olde worlde atmosphere of the cocktail bar. *STB* 👑 👑 👑.

LOMOND HILLS HOTEL,
High Street, Freuchie,
Fife KY7 7EY

Tel: 0337 57329/57498/58180

Accommodation (25 bedrooms, all with private bathroom); Free house; Historic interest; Luncheons, dinners and snacks; Car park (30); Glenrothes 4 miles.

In former times courtiers from nearby Falkland Palace were banished to Freuchie when they fell from favour, but it is such a picturesque village that the punishment must have been easily borne. Those in self-imposed exile here today will find guest accommodation at the Lomond Hills to be of a high standard, with prettily decorated bedrooms (mostly en suite) having television, radio, tea and coffee facilities and telephone, and a most comfortable private lounge provided for residents. The Auld Alliance is kept alive in the elegant restaurant, where Scottish specialities appear alongside some superb French flambé dishes on the à la carte menu. *STB* 👑 👑 👑 👑.

THE PEAT INN,
Peat Inn, By Cupar,
Fife KY15 5LH

Tel: 033-484 206

Accommodation (8 bedrooms, all with private bathroom); Historic interest; Luncheons and dinners; Car park; St. Andrews 6 miles, Cupar 6.

One is not surprised to learn that Chef-Proprietor David Wilson was created Chef Laureate in 1986 by the British Gastronomic Academy, for the dishes presented at this unique establishment would rival those of any restaurant in the world. Accommodation here is on a par with cuisine. Eight individually furnished top-class suites cater for the privileged overnight guest, each one with luxury, fully fitted bathroom, comfortable sitting room with colour television, up-to-the-minute magazines and fresh fruit, and splendid bedroom offering a choice of double, king-size or twin beds. All of the major credit cards are accepted and the accommodation rate includes continental breakfast served in the suite.

Inverness-shire

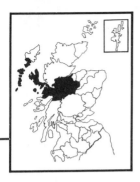

Stage House Inn · Glenfinnan

THE STAGE HOUSE,
Glenfinnan,
Inverness-shire PH37 4LT

Tel: 039-783 246

Accommodation (9 bedrooms, all with private shower/bathroom); Dinners and snacks; Car park (25); Kinlochleven 35 miles, Fort William 15.

One need not fear the sometimes capricious Scottish climate when staying at this appealing seventeenth-century coaching inn, for within its sturdy walls all is cosy and comfortable. Personally run by the proprietors, the Stage House offers attractively furnished guest accommodation, with electric blankets, tea-makers and en suite facilities. Cuisine in the "Taste of Scotland" restaurant is of a high standard, much use being made of wholesome local produce, with salmon, venison, shellfish and lobster when available. Extensive fishing rights on Loch Shiel are owned by the inn, and deer stalking and pony trekking can be arranged. *STB* ♛ ♛ ♛ *Commended, Taste of Scotland.*

Please mention
Recommended WAYSIDE INNS
when seeking refreshment or
accommodation at a Hotel
mentioned in these pages

INVERGARRY HOTEL,
Invergarry,
Inverness-shire PH35 4HG

Tel: 08093 206

Accommodation (10 bedrooms, all with private bathroom); Free house; Historic interest; Dinners and snacks; Car park (20); Inverness 40 miles, Fort William 25, Aonach Mor 22, Loch Ness 7.

Invergarry Hotel, a distinctive Victorian building, is situated on the A87, near the junction with the A82 Fort William-Inverness road, making it an ideal base for exploring the Scottish Highlands. All the comfortable bedrooms have private bathroom, colour television, direct-dial telephone, hairdryer and tea/coffee making facilities. Central heating throughout. Breakfast and dinner are served in the spacious dining room, using the best of local Scottish produce. The hotel is fully licensed. Bar food is available; also snacks and meals in the nearby self-service restaurant. The hotel is privately owned and under the personal supervision of Robert MacCallum, whose aim is to provide a friendly family atmosphere in comfortable surroundings. *STB* 👑 👑 👑 *Commended.*

LOCHAILORT INN,
Lochailort,
Inverness-shire PH38 4LZ

Tel: 068 77 208

Accommodation (7 bedrooms); Free house; Historic interest; Dinners and snacks; Car park; Arisaig 10 miles.

Though popular with the walking, fishing and shooting fraternity you really don't need a surfeit of energy to stay at this cosy Highland hotel, for those seeking simply rest and relaxation are as well catered for as their more active fellows. Here in this outstandingly beautiful corner of the Western Highlands, served by the famous West Highland railway, history comes alive and one almost feels oneself slipping back to the days when Bonnie Prince Charlie raised his standard in 1745. Guest accommodation is comfortable, and in addition to an excellent dinner menu, bar snacks, suppers and lunches are good value for money and will satisfy an appetite sharpened by the clear pure air of this peaceful yet easily accessible region.

TOMICH HOTEL,
Tomich, By Beauly,
Inverness-shire IV4 7LY

Tel: 04565 399

Accommodation (8 bedrooms, all with private bathroom); Free house; Dinners and snacks; Car park; Beauly 1 mile.

Set in the conservation village of Tomich within walking distance of Glen Affric, this superb Highland hotel has retained all the grace and charm of its Victorian origins whilst recent refurbishment has provided all bedrooms with en suite facilities, colour television, tea trays, electric blankets and duvets. There are eight bedrooms, three of which are in the old stable block across the lamplit courtyard. The well-furnished public rooms provide a comfortable residents' lounge, two traditionally styled dining rooms and a delightful bar with oak beams, wood panelling and restful lighting. Good bar meals are available here throughout the day, though in summer visitors may prefer to take their drinks into the sheltered courtyard or out onto the lawns beside the ornamental duckpond. In the dining rooms an excellent à la carte menu is offered in addition to the residents' menu which is intentionally limited and features local produce such as salmon, trout, Scotch lamb, venison and beef. The hotel specialises in fishing and walking holidays and will be pleased to supply details. Guests of the hotel are at liberty to use the swimming pool at nearby Guisachan Farm, which is under the same ownership and also offers self-catering accommodation. *STB* 👑 👑 👑 👑 *Commended.*

NETHER LOCHABER HOTEL,
Onich, Fort William,
Inverness-shire PH33 6SE
Tel: 085-53 235

Accommodation (5 bedrooms); Free house; Historic interest; Luncheons, dinners and snacks; Car park, garages (2); Edinburgh 121 miles, Glasgow 91, Oban 48, Fort William 10.

An ideal centre from which to explore Lochaber, the Ardnamurchan Peninsula and Glencoe. This old Highland inn may be small, but it is a homely place which has been run by the MacKintosh family since 1923. Traditional home cooking goes hand in hand with homely service and comfortable accommodation and private facilities. The inn stands on the shores of beautiful Loch Linnhe at Corran Ferry.

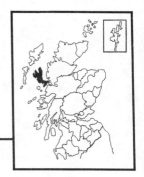

Isle of Skye

FERRY INN,
Uig,
Isle of Skye IV51 9XP
Tel: 047 042 242

Accommodation (6 bedrooms, all with private bathroom); Dinners and snacks; Car park (12); Dunvegan 26 miles, Portree 16.

Local fishermen home from the sea mingle with tourists in the bars of this well-kept little inn, set high above the harbour and offering enchanting views of the ferry as it makes off on its journey to the outer isles of the Hebrides. Good bar lunches and snacks are served between noon and 2.00 pm, and residents and visitors may choose from an à la carte menu in the evening. Comfortable bedrooms (all with private bathroom) have tea-making facilities provided, and guest accommodation is completed by a well-furnished lounge with colour television. Central heating ensures year-round comfort.

Kincardineshire

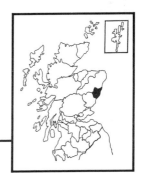

THE ALMA HOTEL (THE OLDE COACH HOUSE),
Alma Place, Laurencekirk,
Kincardineshire AB3 1AL
Tel: 05617 744

Accommodation (6 bedrooms, 3 with private facilities/shower); Free house; Historic interest; High teas, dinners and snacks; Car park; Brechin 10 miles.

This family-run old coaching inn is situated in the charming "Howe O' The Mearns" market town of Laurencekirk. It is an ideal centre for exploring mountains, coast, countryside and the many interesting towns and villages in this part of Scotland. The coast is just seven miles away, and there are stately homes, a nature reserve, fishing, golf and a distillery all within easy reach. All rooms are centrally heated; colour television and tea/coffee making facilities. Excellent home-cooked food is offered in the restaurant and bar, complemented by a selection of ales and fine wines. Children and pets are welcome. Fax services are available for business persons. Self-catering chalets now available. *AA/RAC Listed.*

Lanarkshire

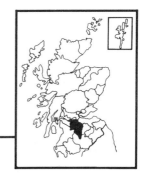

THE CRICKLEWOOD,
27 Hamilton Road, Bothwell,
Lanarkshire
Tel: 0698 853172 Fax: 0698 854672

Accommodation (4 bedrooms); Historic interest; Luncheons, dinners and snacks; Car park (30); Stirling 27 miles, Glasgow 11.

The Cricklewood is famed locally for the quality of its well-kept real ales and of its delicious yet reasonably priced food. Visitors to this friendly little hotel in the lovely conservation village of Bothwell will soon see why. The cosy little lounge bar has a good choice of beers to suit any enthusiast, while the extensive menu will surely contain something to satisfy the choosiest of patrons. Meals are served in the bar and in the restaurant and conservatory, all day every day from 11am to 11pm. Bothwell is within easy reach of both Glasgow and Edinburgh, and with bed and full Scottish breakfast available at the Cricklewood, this makes an excellent base for touring.

Peeblesshire

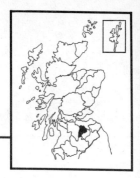

CROOK INN,
Tweedsmuir,
Peebles-shire ML12 6QN
Tel: 089 97 272

Accommodation (7 bedrooms, all with private bathroom); Free house; Historic interest; Dinners and snacks; Car park; Broughton 8 miles.

Robert Burns wrote his poem "Willie Wastle's Wife" in the kitchen of this inspiring hostelry, which has played host to Covenanter and cattle reiver as well as poet in its four-hundred-year history. Situated in attractive gardens in the upper Tweed Valley, seven guest bedrooms cater for those who would stay to savour the peace of this once-violent countryside. All have en suite facilities and are furnished comfortably and with charm, and a good breakfast is included in accommodation charge. A varied and pleasing bar menu is presented at lunchtime and substantial evening dinners are served. The name, please note, refers to the shepherd's staff, not a member of the criminal classes. *AA and RAC**, Egon Ronay, Michelin, Good Food Guide, Good Pub Guide, CAMRA.*

Perthshire

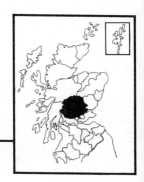

BEIN INN,
Glenfarg,
Perthshire PH2 9PY
Tel: 05773 216

Accommodation (14 bedrooms, all with private bathroom); Historic interest; Luncheons, dinners and snacks; Car park; Edinburgh 33 miles, St. Andrews 28, Dundee 27, Perth 11.

Just off the M90, the Bein Inn nestles in beautiful Glenfarg. Traditional, comfortable and full of atmosphere, the hotel boasts a fine à la carte menu and wine list. The bedrooms, all with private bathrooms, are comfortable, bright and modern. Edinburgh, Perth and Dundee are all within a short drive, and the situation is a golfer's paradise with several famous courses nearby. Opportunities for fishing and shooting abound, together with many other sporting activities. Bargain breaks operate in autumn and spring. Brochure and tariff may be had on request from Mike and Elsa Thompson who will personally supervise your comfort. *STB ♕ ♕ ♕, AA**, Taste of Scotland Recommended.*

BRIDGE OF CALLY HOTEL,
By Blairgowrie,
Perthshire PH10 7JJ

Tel: 025-086 231

Accommodation (9 bedrooms, 6 with private bathroom); Free house; Historic interest; Luncheons, dinners and snacks; Car park (40); Perth 20 miles, Pitlochry 19, Blairgowrie 5.

A former coaching inn overlooking the River Ardle in the unspoilt village of Bridge of Cally, deep in the heart of the magnificent Perthshire countryside. Superb facilities abound for the lovers of country sports such as fishing (the hotel owns rights on the River Ardle and can arrange fishing on the River Ericht), skiing, golf, pony trekking and walking. However there are many other leisure interests including theatres at Perth and Pitlochry, Blair Drummond Wildlife Park and Glamis Castle to name but a few. Warm, comfortable accommodation, superb food and courteous service in this peaceful, friendly hostelry will complete your Highland welcome. *STB* ♛ ♛ ♛ *Commended; AA, RAC; Les Routiers Recommended.*

BRIDGE OF LOCHAY HOTEL,
Killin,
Perthshire FK21 8TS

Tel: 05672 272

Accommodation (17 bedrooms, 7 with private bathroom); Free house; Historic interest; Luncheons, dinners and snacks; Car park (40), garages (3); Glasgow 55 miles, Aberfeldy 22, Lochearnhead 8.

We visited Killin in the autumn when the trees around the famous Falls of Dochart were at their most glorious, but every season brings a new enchantment in this especially lovely area, an ideal centre for touring as well as for salmon and trout fishing on nearby Loch Tay and the River Lochay on whose banks the charming, whitewashed hotel stands. Both table d'hôte and à la carte menus are offered in the fine restaurant, and good substantial bar lunches and suppers are served. Guestrooms, some with private bath or shower, are well appointed and comfortable and have facilities for making tea and coffee. Hosts Frank and Margaret Ogilvie have been in the hotel business for thirty years.

KILLIECRANKIE HOTEL,
By Pitlochry,
Perthshire PH16 5LG

Tel: 0796 3220

Accommodation (12 bedrooms, 10 with private bathroom); Free house; Luncheons, dinners and snacks; Car park (30); Edinburgh 69 miles, Braemar 40, Perth 37, Crieff 34, Blairgowrie 23.

Red squirrels, roe deer and capercaillie are frequent visitors to the wooded grounds of this former dower house, owned and run by the Anderson family with the help of a well chosen staff. Natural pine furniture and matching Laura Ashley fabrics give a homely and pretty air to the guest rooms, most of which have private facilities, and added comfort is provided by electric blankets and heated towel rails. The best of Scottish produce, skilfully prepared by imaginative chefs, is served in the locally popular restaurant, and good bar lunches and suppers attract passing custom as well as a more regular clientele.

LION AND UNICORN,
Thornhill,
Perthshire FK8 3PJ
Tel: 078-685 204

Accommodation (4 bedrooms); Free house; Historic interest; Luncheons, dinners and snacks; Car park (20); Dunblane 7 miles.

Some say Perthshire is at its most beautiful in the autumn, and a cosy base from which to discover its out-of-season charm is provided in this 300-year-old inn, where a log-burning stove adds cheer as well as additional warmth to the convivial lounge. Bedrooms are well-appointed and offer a good standard of comfort, and wholesome meals and snacks may be enjoyed in the bar if the more formal services of the restaurant are not required. Darts and dominoes are played in the public bar, and the Lion and Unicorn has the unusual amenity of its own private bowling green.

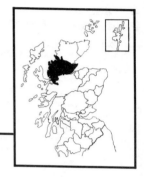

Ross-shire

ACHNASHEEN HOTEL,
Achnasheen,
Ross-shire IV22 2EF
Tel: 044-588 243

Accommodation (18 bedrooms, 6 with private bathroom); Historic interest; Luncheons, dinners and snacks; Car park; Ullapool 48 miles, Beauly 31, Dingwall 30, Garve 16.

If you dream of escaping to a world of clear, cold lochs, of stunning waterfalls and towering peaks, of miles of empty beaches and heather-clad hills, then remote Wester Ross is your dream come true. Experience genuine Highland hospitality at this small, family-owned and managed hotel halfway between Inverness and the coast. The diningroom offers good, plain cooking featuring local venison, salmon and sea trout, together with local produce when available. Bedrooms are well appointed and all offer hot drinks facilities, electric blankets and central heating; open fires augment the cheery warmth of the public rooms in winter.

DUNDONNELL HOTEL,
Dundonnell, By Garve,
Ross-shire IV23 2QR

Tel: 085 483 204
Fax: 085 483 366

Accommodation (24 bedrooms, all with private bathroom); Free house; Dinners and snacks; Car park (60); Ullapool 26 miles.

The Florence family took over the Dundonnell some thirty years ago when it was but a modest country inn huddling in the shelter of the An Teallach mountain range and overlooking Loch Broom. While many would have relied upon that superb setting alone to attract business, this dedicated band have poured all their time and skill and energies into creating here a retreat which offers glorious comfort and first class cuisine as well as an atmosphere of unhurried grace and charm. Twenty-four carefully decorated bedrooms provide accommodation for visitors. All are en suite and have tea and coffee facilities, colour television, telephone and hairdryer, and central heating and electric blankets ensure that out-of-season guests are kept cosy and warm. Parties of four, however, may care to take advantage of the lochside suites, two self-contained two-bedroom apartments, one of which is on the ground floor and admirably suited to the disabled. Dinner at the Dundonnell is an experience to be anticipated, savoured, and remembered with much satisfaction, but those who must forgo the delights of the restaurant will find bar suppers provided in the Broombeg Bar. Tea and homebaking is available throughout the day, and good bar lunches are also served. *STB* 👑 👑 👑 👑 *Commended, AA and RAC***.*

ROYAL HOTEL,
Fortrose,
Ross-shire IV10 8SU

Tel: 0381 20236

Accommodation (10 bedrooms, 5 with private bathroom); Children welcome; Car park; Inverness 16 miles.

Eoin and Jean MacLennan welcome you to their Victorian hotel in the conservation village of Fortrose, only 20 minutes' beautiful drive from the Highland capital of Inverness. Choose peace or conviviality — meet the locals in our old-fashioned public bar and enjoy our freshly cooked local produce. Comfortable bedrooms, lounge and public bar, diningroom and attractive residents' lounge. Open January to December. Please contact Mrs MacLennan for details. *STB* 👑 👑 👑 *Commended.*

THE OLD INN,
Gairloch,
Ross-shire IV21 2BD

Tel: 0445 2006

Accommodation (14 bedrooms, all with private bathroom); Free house; Historic interest; Dinners and snacks; Car park (50); Inverness 71 miles, Ullapool 56.

The famous gardens of Inverewe are just seven miles from this solid and welcoming family-run inn, and guests booking for three nights' dinner, bed and breakfast may visit them free of charge. Real ales are a speciality, and good bar food is served here daily. Both table d'hôte and à la carte menus are offered in the dining room, locally caught seafood, trout and salmon vying for the gourmet's attention with fine Aberdeen Angus beef and skilfully prepared venison. Colour television, beverage makers, direct-dial telephones and child/baby listening facilities are provided in each of the en suite guestrooms, all of which are furnished for comfort as well as being pleasing to the eye. *STB* 👑 👑 👑 *Commended, AA/RAC **.*

MOREFIELD MOTEL,
North Road, Ullapool,
Ross-shire IV26 2TH

Tel: 0854 2161
Fax: 0854 2870

Accommodation (11 bedrooms, all with private bathroom); Free house; Dinners and snacks; Car park (60); Dingwall 47 miles.

Modern chalet-type accommodation is to be found at this privately owned establishment in the bustling and quaint fishing port of Ullapool, and all rooms have either bath or shower en suite and facilities for making tea and coffee, as well as fresh, attractive decor and supremely comfortable beds. A comprehensive selection of fare is available in the bar, ranging from light snacks to lobster and steak meals substantial enough for appetites sharpened by Highland air, and for those who would choose to dine intimately and with just a touch of formality, the à la carte restaurant is noted for its wonderful range of seafood and steak dishes. 🌸🌸🌸, *Good Food Guide, Good Pub Guide.*

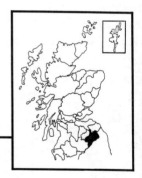

Roxburghshire

BUCCLEUCH ARMS HOTEL,
St Boswells,
Roxburghshire TD6 0EW

Tel: 0835 22243 Fax: 0835 23965

Accommodation (18 bedrooms, 17 with private bathroom); Free house; Historic interest; Luncheons, dinners and snacks; Car park (70); Melrose 4 miles.

Buccleuch Arms is a privately owned hotel in the Scottish Borders. There are many places of historic interest to visit; golf and fishing close by. Bar food is served from 12 noon and lunch can be taken in the restaurant. Dinner is served from 6pm. Most rooms have private facilities, colour television and telephone. Relax in the evenings by the open fire and enjoy the warm, friendly Scottish hospitality. *STB* 🌸🌸🌸🌸 *Commended.*

Selkirkshire

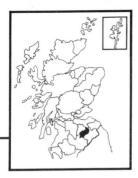

"A BIT WREN'S NEST"

TIBBIE SHIELS INN,
St Mary's Loch,
Selkirkshire TD7 5NE
Tel: 0750 42231

Accommodation (5 bedrooms); Free house; Historic interest; High teas, dinners and snacks; Car park (30); Selkirk 13 miles.

The history of this idyllically situated inn is much too involved to dwell on here, but those interested in the redoubtable Tibbie will find a pamphlet available which tells the full story and dispels any illusions that women's lib was unheard of before the 1960s. Wholesome and tasty bar meals are served from 12.30 pm right through until 8.30 pm, and a full dinner menu is presented in the restaurant from 6.00 pm nightly. Guest accommodation comprises three double rooms, one twin and one family, all spick and span and comfortably furnished, and residents have the opportunity to fish free of charge on St Mary's Loch. *STB ♥, AA Listed, Good Pub Guide, Ashley Courtenay.*

GORDON ARMS HOTEL,
Yarrow,
Selkirkshire
Tel: 0750 82222

Accommodation (6 bedrooms); Free house; Historic interest; Dinners and snacks; Car park; Selkirk 13 miles.

Ramble here and find good cheer! The Gordon Arms Hotel is an hotel of historic interest, situated amidst some of the best walking terrain and scenery to be found. It is also ideally placed for fishing on the rivers Tweed, Yarrow and Ettrick. It has changed little since the days when it was the meeting place of Sir Walter Scott and James Hogg, "The Ettrick Shepherd". Bar lunches and bar suppers from a comprehensive menu are served daily. High teas are available from Easter to the end of October. Bunkhouse accommodation specifically for walkers and cyclists is also available. Real ales are served and there are 46 malt whiskies to choose from.

Wigtownshire

STEAM PACKET INN,
Harbour Row, Isle of Whithorn,
Wigtownshire DG8 8LL
Tel: 098-85 334

Accommodation (5 bedrooms, all with private bathroom); Free house; Historic interest; Luncheons, dinners and snacks; Newton Stewart 22 miles, Wigtown 15.

Though small in size, this attractive quayside hotel run by John Scoular and his wife has a reputation which stretches far beyond the picturesque little town it graces. Overnight accommodation is available in spick and span, nicely furnished guestrooms, complete with beverage-making facilities, colour television and private bathroom, and the bed and breakfast charge is agreeably modest. Food is well prepared, plentiful and also moderately priced, and can be served in the beamed diningroom or in the bar which looks out over the yachts and fishing boats which frequent the pretty harbour. Residents have free access to golf on the local course.

CROWN HOTEL,
North Crescent, Portpatrick,
Wigtownshire DG9 8SX
Tel: 0776 81 261

Accommodation (12 bedrooms, all with private bathroom); Free house; Luncheons, dinners and snacks; Stranraer 6 miles.

Seafood is a particular speciality of this fine, family-run hotel – hardly surprising as it is only a few steps from the water's edge, facing westwards over the harbour of enchanting Portpatrick village to the Irish Channel beyond. Fresh caught crab, lobster, prawns and scallops are on offer in the bar, together with the usual steaks and sandwiches, and the pleasant thirties-style restaurant caters amply for more formal dining. A gracious conservatory opens on to sheltered, well-planned gardens, and guest accommodation is attractively furnished and comfortable in the extreme, all rooms having en suite facilities and television.

Please mention
Recommended WAYSIDE INNS
when seeking refreshment or
accommodation at a Hotel
mentioned in these pages

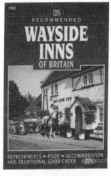

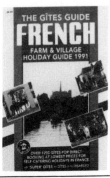

ONE FOR YOUR FRIEND 1991

FHG Publications have a large range of attractive holiday accommodation guides for all kinds of holiday opportunities throughout Britain. They also make useful gifts at any time of year. Our guides are available in most bookshops and larger newsagents but we will be happy to post you a copy direct if you have any difficulty. We will also post abroad but have to charge separately for post or freight.

The inclusive cost of posting and packing the guides to you or your friends in the UK is as follows:

Farm Holiday Guide
ENGLAND, WALES and IRELAND
Board, Self-catering, Caravans/Camping,
Activity Holidays. About 600 pages. **£3.60**

Farm Holiday Guide SCOTLAND
All kinds of holiday accommodation. **£2.60**

SELF-CATERING & FURNISHED
HOLIDAYS
Over 1000 addresses throughout for
Self-catering and caravans in Britain. **£3.00**

BRITAIN'S BEST HOLIDAYS
A quick-reference general guide
for all kinds of holidays. **£2.50**

The FHG Guide to CARAVAN &
CAMPING HOLIDAYS
Caravans for hire, sites and
holiday parks and centres. **£2.60**

BED AND BREAKFAST STOPS
Over 1000 friendly and comfortable
overnight stops. **£3.00**

CHILDREN WELCOME! FAMILY
HOLIDAY GUIDE
Family holidays with details of
amenities for children and babies. **£2.50**

Recommended SHORT BREAK
HOLIDAYS IN BRITAIN
'Approved' accommodation for quality bargain
breaks. Introduced by John Carter. **£3.50**

Recommended COUNTRY HOTELS
OF BRITAIN
Including Country Houses, for
the discriminating. **£3.50**

Recommended WAYSIDE INNS
OF BRITAIN
Pubs, Inns and small hotels. **£3.50**

PGA GOLF GUIDE
Where to play and where to stay
Over 2000 golf courses with convenient
accommodation. Endorsed by the PGA. **£6.50**

PETS WELCOME!
The unique guide for holidays for
pet owners and their pets. **£3.00**

BED AND BREAKFAST IN BRITAIN
Over 1000 choices for touring and
holidays throughout Britain. **£2.50**

LONDON'S BEST BED AND
BREAKFAST HOTELS
Inspected and recommended with prices. Over 120
safe, clean and friendly small hotels. **£3.25**

THE FRENCH FARM AND VILLAGE
HOLIDAY GUIDE
The official guide to self-catering
holidays in the 'Gîtes de France'. **£7.50**

Tick your choice and send your order and payment to FHG PUBLICATIONS, ABBEY MILL BUSINESS CENTRE, SEEDHILL, PAISLEY PA1 1JN (TEL: 041-887 0428. FAX: 041-889 7204). **Deduct** 10% for 2/3 titles or copies; 20% for 4 or more.

Send to: NAME ....

ADDRESS ....

....

.... POST CODE ....

I enclose Cheque/Postal Order for £ ....

SIGNATURE .... DATE ....

MAP
SECTION

The following seven pages of maps indicate the main
cities, towns and holiday centres of Britain. Space
obviously does not permit every location featured in
this book to be included but the approximate position
may be ascertained by using the distance indications
quoted and the scale bars on the maps.

Map 1

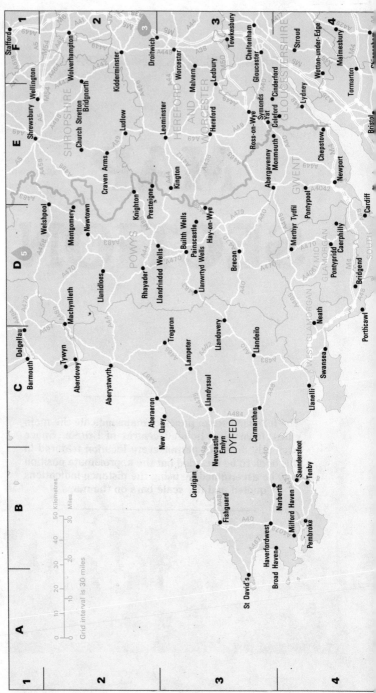

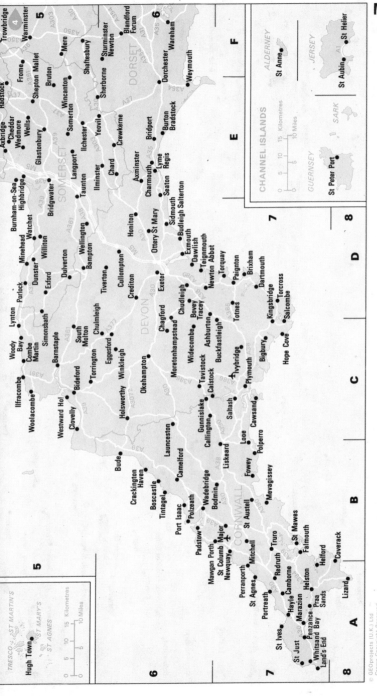

Map 2

Map 3

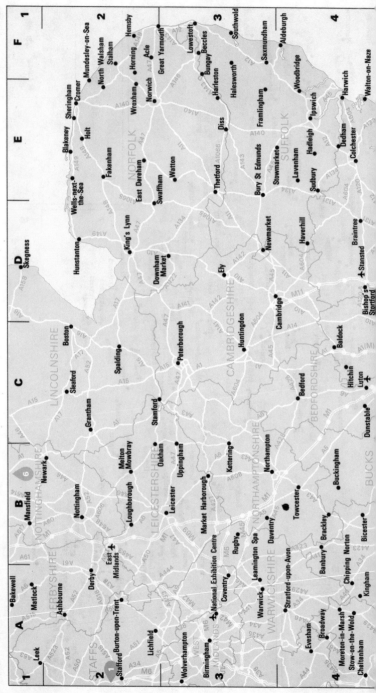

Map 4

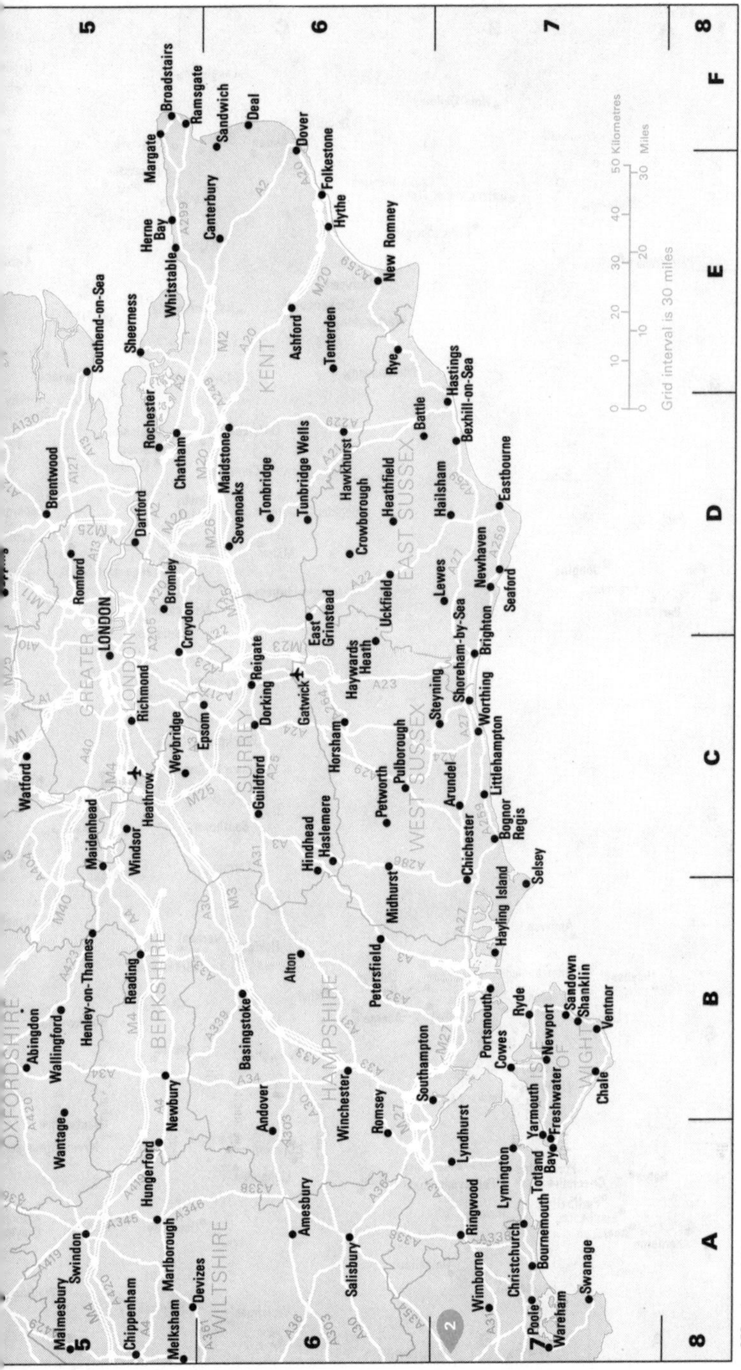

Grid interval is 30 miles

50 Kilometres
30 Miles

© GEOprojects (U.K.) Ltd
Crown Copyright Reserved

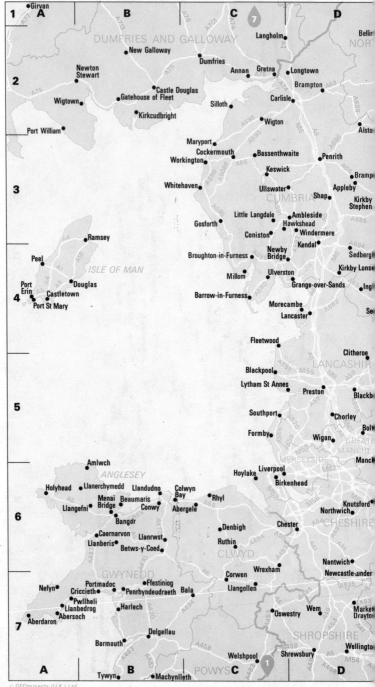

Map 5

Map 6

E F G H

1

Morpeth

Whitley Bay
Tynemouth
South Shields

MBERLAND

Corbridge
Newcastle-upon-Tyne
xham
Sunderland

2

Durham

DURHAM

Bishop Auckland
Middleton-in-Teesdale
Middlesbrough
Redcar
Saltburn-by-the-Sea

Barnard Castle
Darlington
Guisborough
Whitby

CLEVELAND

Stokesley

Richmond

3

Leyburn
Northallerton
Scarborough

Middleham
Thirsk
Helmsley
Pickering
Filey

NORTH YORKSHIRE
Flamborough

Ripon
Castle Howard
Malton
Sledmere
Bridlington

Grassington
Driffield

Skipton
Harrogate
Hornsea

4

Keighley
Ilkley
York

Bingley
Selby
Beverley

Bradford
Leeds
HUMBERSIDE

Heptonstall
Halifax
Hull

WEST YORKSHIRE

Huddersfield
Goole

5

Barnsley
Doncaster
Scunthorpe
Grimsby
Cleethorpes

SOUTH YORKSHIRE

Glossop
Gainsborough
Louth
Mablethorpe

Sheffield
Alford

Buxton
Worksop
sfield
Bakewell
Chesterfield
Lincoln
Horncastle
Skegness

ton
Leek
Matlock
Mansfield

DERBYSHIRE
NOTTINGHAM-SHIRE
LINCOLNSHIRE

6

Ashbourne
Newark
Sleaford
Boston

-on-Trent
Nottingham

Derby
Grantham

East Midlands
A52

FFORDSHIRE

afford
Burton-upon-Trent
Loughborough
Melton Mowbray
Spalding

7

Lichfield
LEICESTERSHIRE
Stamford

Leicester
Oakham
Uppingham
Peterborough

E F G H

Scale: 0 10 20 30 40 50 Kilometres
0 10 20 30 Miles
Grid interval is 30 miles

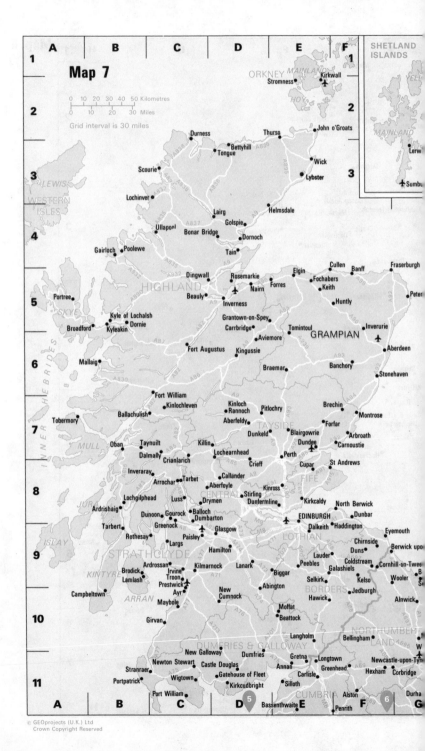